THINK SMARTER

DO LESS GET MORE

From Your Business AND Your Life

Andy Hemming

Chameleon
Business Press

Published by Chameleon Business Press

ISBN 978-1-5272-7322-1

Contents

Endorsements

"If there is one thing Andy is known for in the ActionCOACH community, it's thinking smarter and doing less whilst achieving world class results for himself and more importantly his clients.

His whole philosophy is about you being better so you can help others be better too. And it works. The level of results and satisfaction his clients experience, both in terms of business improvement and increased freedom are testament to everything you will learn in this book.

Andy has put together a succinct reflection of his strategies and philosophy. Use this book, make notes, it's a step by step guide to help you, then your team think smarter, become more efficient and effective, and then structure your business to create alignment and engagement.

In turn, that will lead you to a business in which everyone, because they are pulling in the same direction, creates more: more profit, more freedom, and more impact on the marketplace you serve.

The lessons you take from this book will lead you to more satisfaction and freedom as the business owner. And that is the goal … right …?
Because being in business should give you more life."

– Brad Sugars, Founder and CEO, ActionCOACH

"A book that will truly change the way you view your work and life! Andy has written an inspiring and practical guide on creating the work-life balance you crave — one that will give you the freedom to focus on the people that matter, while continuing to succeed in your business".

– Marshall Goldsmith, New York Times #1 bestselling author of Triggers, Mojo, and What Got You Here Won't Get You There.

"Lots of gain for no pain! A practical, step-by-step guide to having more success, fun and fulfilment - using simple, quick and proven techniques. Want more success? Just follow Andy's process. It works!'

– Andy Bounds, Sales expert, award-winning consultant and bestselling author

"This book punches well above its weight. And it does punch: it will make you take your dreams seriously, confront your fears and doubts and push you to action. It's fact-full, practical and uplifting: a brilliant guide and handbook for the aspiring business owner'

– Myles Downey, Author 'Effective Modern Coaching' and 'Enabling Genius'; Coach

About the Author

Andy Hemming is the senior partner of ActionCOACH Black Country, a business coaching firm which serves businesses in and around the Black Country area of the West Midlands. He has won the UK award for the Highest Client Satisfaction Rating for the last four years in succession and the firm ranks as the number one business coaching firm in the UK and the Europe.

Since Andy began his coaching business in 2007, he has personally worked with hundreds of businesses of all sizes and across all sectors to help them grow their businesses and gain more freedom in their lives.

To find out more, visit:
https://blackcountry.actioncoach.co.uk

Author Preface

On Thursday 3rd May 2007, as I walked through the Mailbox shopping centre in Birmingham, my phone rang, and my life changed. The call was from ActionCOACH, the world's number one coaching organisation. I learned of the opportunity to have my own business. Not only could I determine my own work/life balance, but I'd have the privilege of helping people to develop and transform their lives while continuously developing my own skills.

All of my core values in one place.

Just two months later, on Friday 6th July 2007, I boarded the plane to Las Vegas for my 10-day induction training with a very clear intention: to have a great business *and* a great life *and* go on a journey with myself and my clients to help us all transform our lives beyond what we originally thought possible.

It was always my vision to turn my business into a professional services firm. I'm on that journey now. But, up to the end of 2018, I worked a maximum of three days per week which left a whole two days for myself and two days for my family. I achieved a highly time leveraged business which performs in the top 1% of our esteemed ActionCOACH community of 1,500 plus franchise partners in (at the time of writing) over 90 countries. It seems highly fitting at this point to offer my sincere gratitude to Brad Sugars, our founder and chairman, who was visionary enough over 25 years ago to create not only the organisation that I am proud to be a part of, but also the foundations for the learnings on which I have built my own self-education and business.

It's allowed me to have fun and freedom in my business, on my own, and with my family as well as personal fulfilment in my own development. For that, I'm both immensely grateful and proud in equal measure.

The thoughts I'm about to share with you are the result of my learning since 2007, and how I've made that happen, not only for me, but also for my clients. I've taken the brilliant ActionCOACH system, heaped learning upon learning on top, and had the immense privilege of sharing the journey of some incredible people. Of course, I don't expect you to agree with all of these learnings. They're my opinion at the time of writing and I'm sure that they will adapt and evolve as I learn new things and experience different situations. All I ask is that you are open-minded enough to consider them because, when you do, it may catalyse a new thought and a new action, even if you don't agree with the original idea. These hard-won insights are borne of my experiences with hundreds of businesses, including my own, both in good times and in bad.

During that journey, there've been some tough times (as it is for all of us) and, as we all know, those are testing. We need support and encouragement to get through them. That's the reason that I'm dedicating this book to my fabulous wife, Kate, who has been my rock for the last 25 years. Without her, I wouldn't have achieved this, and for her love and support, I am eternally grateful and blessed. It's also for my kids, Oliver and Alex, who teach me lessons about myself on a daily basis and make me immensely proud.

Lastly, this book is dedicated to you. The person who wants to escape the treadmill in favour of achieving freedom in your business and freedom of choice in your life but aren't quite sure how.

I wish you every success on your journey.

Andy Hemming
September 2020

Prologue

"Dad, tell us a story, pleeease..." Alex, my 7-year-old's plea jolted me back into the crisp, seemingly perfect January morning in 2010. A blue, cloudless sky framed the panorama of open countryside, punctuated only by the gently meandering river. The backdrop of the snow-topped Malvern hills on the horizon completed the chocolate box scene. Underfoot, fresh frost crackled on the frozen grass as we walked, and the biting wind chilled our exposed faces as I, my two sons and our chocolate Labrador walked our usual weekend route. While the dog ran circles around us, nose covered in a sparkling white dusting of frost, waiting expectantly for someone to hurl a stick into the freezing water, my boys' gloved hands tugged gently on mine, insistently trying to coax me into making up a story to pass the time on our walk.

How could life possibly be any better?

But that wasn't the thought going through my mind. Far from it, in fact. At the moment of Alex's plea, I was oblivious to the beauty of my surroundings, and the fact that the only thing that Oliver and Alex needed from me was to be *present*. In that moment, consumed by my own thoughts of worry, self-doubt and admonishment, I was missing all of the most important things in my life. And in that moment, I made a decision; a decision that my life had to change. And the reason was very, very simple: I simply could not carry on like *this*, because *this* was destroying my life. This situation was the furthest thing from my mind in 2007 when I started my business and I could not have imagined that I would have ended up there.

I'm sure I'm not alone when I say that I started my business with the idea of achieving more money and more freedom, to escape the "rat race" and be in control of my own destiny. I'm equally sure that I'm not the only one who has experienced some serious discomfort on that journey. At the moment when Alex jolted me out of my own thoughts, there would have been only one word to describe what I was feeling: panic.

Panic because, in slightly under one week from that date, my mortgage payment was due and, less than one week following that, school fees, and I had no idea how I was going to cover them. My savings were gone, the debts were growing, and I could see no way out. It was perhaps the most uncomfortable I have ever felt. I had hit an all-time low. It was affecting my health and I felt like a dark cloud hung permanently over my head. In the months preceding, I had spent hours sitting at the desk in my office, wondering how I was ever going to fix this situation. Sleepless nights were spent worrying about lack of money, frantically thinking about what I could do to recover from this ever-deepening hole. Fear had consumed me, was controlling me and, as a result, days and weeks were passing me by and I was missing what was happening in my life; missing all of those special things that should not be missed, like weekend walks with my boys in crisp, winter countryside.

But, how did I get *here*? How could my life have gone so wrong? Sure, there had been a recession going on for over a year, but I'd always been tough, always overcome every obstacle that life had thrown at me and come out on top. What made now so different? Why was I making such terrible choices? This was not who I was!

My approach was clearly not working. It had to change, and it had to change radically if I was going to correct the ever-worsening trajectory I found myself on. It was time to think differently, and that's where the turning point came. Because different thoughts create different actions, which in turn create different results. As a consequence of the ideas I'm going to share with you in this book, I have been fortunate enough to change the situation of that cold

January day to achieve a business which affords me both a great business *and* a great life; a business which allows me significant freedom both in my business and my life; a business in which I think *smarter* and work *less*. And I have helped hundreds of other business owners to do the same.

That's the purpose of this book. It's a step-by-step guide to moving towards a business which affords you the life you envisioned when you started (or even something better). It's a collection of ideas, structured in the order that they should be tackled to help you capture that freedom and a streamlined and efficient plan where, if you follow the ideas presented in this book, the nitty gritty will take care of itself.

I'd like to share these ideas with you in the hope that you can take some of them away, embed them in your daily life, and achieve the same for yourself.

Introduction

Your business is a vehicle for your life. If it's running well, its purpose is to transport you quickly and efficiently between where you currently are and where you want to be. Of course, sometimes, as we move further in our journey, the road ahead becomes more visible, so we choose to go further than we initially imagined.

Though many never get that far.

What were your dreams and goals when you started your business?

Did you want more freedom to choose, to make more money, *and* to have personal fulfilment? I imagine so!

What happened?

If you're like many of the business owners I'm fortunate enough to work with, you started your business with ideas like this, and then somehow got consumed in the day-to-day, climbing onto the treadmill and running like hell to keep things going. After years of running (remember a treadmill runs you), you might be feeling a little tired (we call that burnout).

It doesn't have to be that way.

But, if we're going to change our current reality, we first have to change the way that we think. That's the first section of this book, *Thinking Smarter*. I need you to start thinking differently, smarter, about your life and your business, because different thoughts will lead to different questions, new decisions and new actions. In turn, those new actions will bring new results.

We have to start with how we think if we are going to change anything in our life, be that in or out of business, because life is a mirror. Our results are a reflection of how we interact with the world, so we first need to examine what's showing up in our mirror, and check that it's fit for the journey we want to go on. I'll give you the framework to put a smarter way of thinking in place, and then the tools to develop yourself into the person you need to be to achieve your dreams.

Then, in section two, *The Power of Time and Systems,* we'll deal with your two key resources. Time is our only finite resource, so how come most people are so profligate with it? I find it hard to understand why we are, in general, so happy to waste something so precious. Often, I'll experience resistance from people who perceive that what I bring to the table (coaching) will be the straw that breaks the camel's back ("I'm too busy to fit this in right now!"). This most definitely isn't the case, so we need to remove all the excuses around time, and get you thinking differently about how you use it. I'm pretty blunt when I coach, and I call it "doing stupid." This means wasting time on low-value tasks instead of focusing on priorities to fulfil our goals and dreams. By the end of this section, you'll have created the high-performance mindset and learnt the tools to do more with less.

We'll also consider systems, the framework you can implement in your business to create the environment in which your team can perform at the required level to provide your customers with predictable and consistent results. This will allow you to separate yourself from the business of your business and start to allow you to do less and apply more of that smarter thinking.

Once we've learned how to think smarter and do less, our next focus will be section three, the creation of the vehicle which allows you to start *Getting MORE From Your Business and Your Life*. It's the key to business success: having the right team on your bus who want to join you on your journey and know what their part in it is.

There's no point implementing business strategy and operational actions for a team who aren't engaged with you and your business, and the sad fact is that the majority of teams aren't engaged. Great people build a great business, and they're your key to freedom, so we need to talk about how to make the most of them.

Within this section, we'll also discuss some operational aspects of the management of your business which will enable you to have the confidence that it's running as you want it to, whether you are there or not. This isn't an encyclopaedia of business strategies, however. It's the framework which will allow you and your team to perform at their highest level, and so afford you the growth and freedom you want. Because less is *always* more!

I'm writing this not as a "guru", but as someone who has been privileged enough to work with some very committed and talented people who are open to challenge. I've experienced what has worked and not worked for them and from that I've developed this philosophy which I'll share with you. A philosophy which is intended to provoke, motivate and inspire you to reflect and incite dynamic change. The most important thing for you, therefore, is to take the contents of this book in the manner in which they are intended: as an opportunity to break the cycle of your business thinking and consider it from a different perspective.

As we go through the book, I'm going to ask you to stop from time to time and do a short interactive exercise. You'll know when it's that time, as you'll see this symbol:

I'd urge you to do the exercises, as there's no point reading this book and *not* taking action. Remember the organisation that I'm a part of: ActionCOACH!

My sincere hope is that, by the time you've finished reading this book and implementing the strategies, your life and your business will be on a trajectory to a very different place.

THE REALITY OF OWNING A SMALL BUSINESS

It's a constant source of both concern and amazement to me that there are so many business owners out there who choose to operate in the way that they do. By that, I mean that they sacrifice their personal and family life for their business because they believe that, if they work harder, it will all be OK. That, if they just work harder for a couple of years, everything will improve and then they can ease off and enjoy the fruits of their labour.

For most people, that's not why they went into business. They chose this route as it would give them more time and freedom in their life, not less. They wanted to make more money, not wake up at night worried about how to pay the wage bill. And, most certainly, they never went into business to be the person who opens the doors in the morning, closes the doors at night and runs around like the proverbial blue-arsed fly for the hours in-between.

Some go into business to serve some higher purpose and make their part of the world better. In some cases, this comes to fruition. For the most part, however, people just end up working harder.

More is rarely more. When I work with my clients, we will often talk about the concept of "less is more" (hence the title of this book). Success is often about stopping doing things which aren't working and getting really focused on doing more of the things that are, i.e. Doing less to achieve more. As business owners, we should focus our energies on those activities that maximise "bang for your buck".

There is a famous saying: "The definition of insanity is doing the same thing over and over and expecting different results." It's a common business mantra often attributed to Albert Einstein which sums up the importance of innovation and reinvention. To innovate or reinvent requires new knowledge in order to create new actions, which in turn will create new results. The whole process of change, therefore, begins with new thinking.

However, this isn't the thinking of most people who start a business. The more common pattern looks like this: a good electrician starts an electrician business; a good architect starts an architect's practice. They're good at what they do. In fact, they must believe that they're up there amongst the best, or why would they take the risk to abandon the security of their regular income to go and create something for themselves? However, the reality is that they're good electricians or architects, not great businesspeople. The results of that will be explored shortly. Most continue to be great at their chosen profession, but they have to learn the trade of running a business by trial and, usually, a lot of error.

Consequently, time goes by and not much changes in terms of results, but the owner starts to reach burnout and either falls out of love with their business, runs out of energy, runs out of money, or all of the above.

No wonder many of the business owners I speak with aren't where they want to be in their business or life.

But there's something else that's really important: the consequences of these actions rarely lead to a good outcome.

When I look at the business community I now serve, the statistics sadden me greatly. Look at the rates of business births and deaths, which are openly published by the Office for National Statistics. The numbers vary very little year on year, and look something like this:

80% of businesses will fail in the first five years of their life.

80% of what's left will fail in the next five years.

Therefore, the chances of making it to 10 years old are 4%. And guess what the number one reason is for that failure rate?

Lack of knowledge.

But it's not just the reason that businesses fail. It's also the reason that businesses get stuck. I can't tell you the number of business owners who admitted they used to employ staff and have gone back to doing it themselves as it's just easier that way. That's not thinking smarter or doing less, and it's certainly not the route to get more out of your business or life. There's a definite and clearly defined path to those things; and that's what we'll cover in this book.

I've alluded to this earlier, so let me explain in more detail. For the most part, people who start businesses aren't great businesspeople. They're great at doing what they do. For example, a plumber will be great at fixing leaks in a tap, but normally not so great at managing cashflow, understanding accounts, marketing and selling, and managing and leading a team effectively. The problem is, *that* is the work of a business owner. Fixing the leaks is the work of the employees of the business owner.

Just reflect, for a moment, on all of the wasted money, time, energy and emotion wrapped up in that failure rate. Just imagine the impact on all of those families as their livelihood collapses around them.

And consider this. We, the owners of the small and medium-sized businesses, are the ones responsible for growing this economy. Wouldn't it therefore make more sense if we were all more competent at making that happen?

When we first get into a car, we have to have driving lessons. It's the law. We're not allowed out on our own until our level of competence is deemed worthy of being put in charge of a vehicle, sometimes driven at high speed. It's only then that we can single-handedly become responsible for other people's lives because, up until that point, there's normally only the learner and the instructor in the car. And the instructor can put the brakes on if it looks like something is going to go wrong.

Not so in business. Anyone can get into any vehicle to transport any number of people from their current position to another place, without so much as a single instruction from any competent source. For some, it's a pleasant journey. For most, it's a bumpy ride, punctuated by stalls, wrong turns and stops by the roadside to fix the vehicle. And for some, it's just a full-on crash.

I want to share with you my understanding of what being in business means in this book. My hope is that you take some nuggets of my knowledge and implement them in your life and business journey right now to help you drive a better vehicle, more competently.

If you choose to embrace the principles shared here, I *guarantee* you will be more successful!

How can I say that with such confidence?

At the time of writing, we've just completed an externally conducted client satisfaction survey for my coaching business. The statistics speak for themselves:

100% of clients responded to the survey.

62% had at least doubled their turnover since working with me, and 46% had at least doubled their profits.

88% said that their work-life balance had improved. Indeed, 29% said that their free time had increased by up to 50%.

100% recommended coaching, saying that it made a positive difference to their lives.

I need to put this into context: 22% of the respondents were in their *first year* of coaching!

What impact would it have on your life *and* your business if you were to achieve similar results?

OK, let's get going!

Section 1: Thinking Smarter

"The only way it gets better for you is when you get better. Better is not something you wish, it's something you become."
Jim Rohn

Introduction

Everything starts with a thought. Stephen R. Covey, in his book, *The 7 Habits of Highly Effective People*[1] alludes to the fact that everything is created twice: once in the imagination, and once in reality.

It stands to reason then, that if we are going to perform better, then we need to think differently. We need to imagine a new way forward to create something new in reality. That needs a new train of thought and it also probably needs a change in the *way* that we're thinking.

We'll look at a couple of core concepts in the next chapters which will help you to reframe the way you see the world. They'll help you to put aside some of the things that are getting in your way, and determine the changes you need to make in yourself in order to go out and become the person who is capable of achieving your dreams…even if they seem like something unreachable right now.

---

[1] *The 7 Habits of Highly Effective People*, Stephen R. Covey, Simon & Schuster UK, Reissue Edition (21 Nov. 2013)

Chapter 1

The Barriers to Thinking Smarter

INTRODUCTION

Most of us would love to be more successful and perform better in some (or many) areas of our life. Isn't it interesting, though, that when we think about growth, many of us think about *doing* more? In reality, we can only do so much; wouldn't it make more sense to think about how we could *be* better instead?

The clue is in the name: we are human *beings* and not human *doings*!

Of course, in order for us to be better, we may need to start to think differently as some of our thought processes may be getting in the way of the improved performance we're striving for.

In this chapter, we'll look at some models of thinking which will start to form a framework for better quality of thought, which can lead to better quality of decisions and action. In other words, we'll take a good look at the things which cause us to hinder our own performance and progression.

We'll then put some models in place so that you can catch yourself early when those unhelpful thought processes show up. By the end of this chapter, you'll have all the tools you need to open your mind to higher levels of performance in *all* areas of your life.

The First Test: Defining Your Barriers to Success

I've run this exercise in seminars for years now. It relates to personal performance, as I assume that everyone who sits in a seminar, and everyone who reads this book, wants to improve in some way. I use the performance model (figure 1.1, W. Timothy Gallwey[2]).

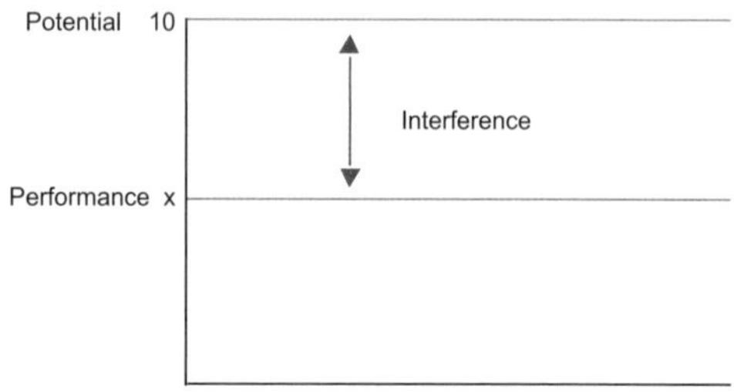

Figure 1.1: The performance model

Think of an area of your life where you'd like to improve your performance. On a scale of 1-10, get a really clear idea of what a 10 would be like. How would you be performing and what results would you be achieving? Write it down. Let's call this your potential.

Now score yourself on your current level of performance. It can't be a 10 because you've said you can improve. We'll call this your performance (X) – write that number down too.

Next, think about what is causing you to lower your score from a 10 to the number at which you've rated your current performance. There may be more than one thing getting in the way but write down the biggest thing. We'll call that interference.

You should now have three things on your piece of paper. A clear idea of what 10 would look like, a clear score of your current performance, and a clear indication of what's causing your score to lower.

The equation is:

Performance = Potential – Interference.

---

[2] *The Inner Game of Tennis*, W. Timothy Gallwey, Pan, 2015

If you are looking to perform better in any area of your life, you'll need to remove the interferences, the stuff that's getting in the way. You'll be able to use this formula again and again in your business to get you and your team to continuously improve performance by systematically identifying and then removing the interferences.

When interferences are removed, there is only one direction that performance can move – up.

We'll come back to this in a moment, but first…

Making Positive Choices: Stay in BED or Grab an OAR

If we're going to achieve better results, then we need to think differently: thoughts cause actions, and actions cause results. Take a look at figure 1.2 below.

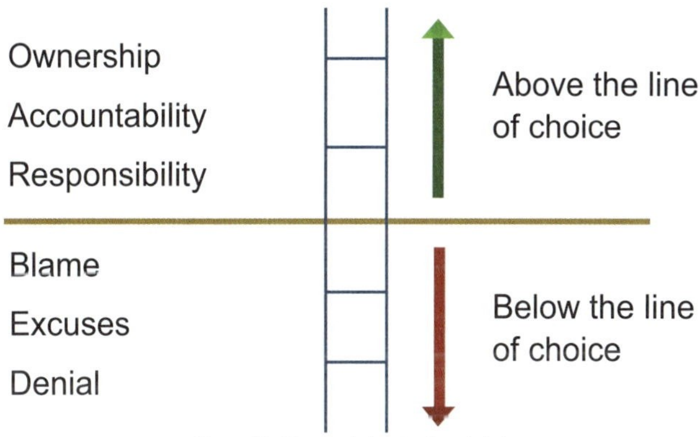

Figure 1.2: Above or below the line of choice

You'll notice there's a line in the middle, separating the two groups of words. Let's call that the "line of choice". You can choose to think and act "above the line" of choice and take ownership, be accountable and responsible, or you can choose to act "below the line" and blame, make excuses or be in denial. Notice the first letter of the above the line choices:

O-A-R: when you choose to act above the line of choice, you will have an *OAR* to steer your own ship, as you're controlling the direction in which you're headed.

High-performance decision-making can only happen when we choose to be above that line.

Look at the first letter of each of the words under the line: B-E-D. That's right! Bed: which is where you may as well stay if you make these choices. After all, you make your *BED* and you lie in it.

And remember, we *choose* each and every one of our reactions.

This simple diagram isn't as simple as it seems, by the way. Instead of being a collection of six words, consider it instead as a ladder.

The first rung is denial. When we choose denial, we are sticking our heads in the sand and hoping it will all go away. Denial is, for example, not looking at the bank balance because it's too frightening and we don't want to remind ourselves how bad things are.

When we choose to come out of denial, the excuses come. "Of course, I didn't have time to look at my bank account, because I was too busy".

As we start to realise that everything that we do is a choice and therefore our excuses don't really stand up, we move towards blame: "My team should be answering the phone and dealing with the customers, but they just don't do it as well as I do". Or, "Of course the bank account looks bad. My customers aren't paying me on time!" Whose fault is that?

Our next choice on the ladder would be to realise that we are the only ones who are responsible, not only for what's in the bank account, but also for how our team deals with our customers. Response-able: the ability to respond. Now we're above that line of choice, so we're starting to decide to *make* things happen rather than *let* them happen. In other words, if I got my team to deal with customers how I wanted them to, I would have the time to check the bank account and start to do something about it. It's now obvious we need to make a different choice if things are going to change as we can't continue to blame others for our results.

The recognition of this responsibility is positive. But, if we're going to change something, we have to start recording it so that we know whether it's improving, deteriorating or staying the same. There's an old adage: "What gets measured gets managed". That's accountability – we are now starting to *count* and record our actions. This means we can actually start to see the impact of those actions and therefore make better decisions around the results. For example, we'd want to measure how the team deals with customers to ensure that clients are as satisfied as when *we* dealt with them. We'd also want to measure our levels of outstanding debt to see if our conversations with customers were improving the situation.

Now we are starting to create ownership. Ownership means that, because we are measuring our results, and the results that we want to achieve are clear, you and your team have enough clarity to take actions to move you towards those results. If everyone knows what they are responsible for, and the measures are clear, then of course ownership is easily achievable.

Choosing to operate below the line of choice isn't an unusual response. There's always a convincing reason to go below: COVID-19, Brexit, recession, and the list will inevitably go on.

Let's consider the economic environment since 2008. Of course, there have been economic cycles similar to the cycle we're in now, but I'm just using this period for illustrative purposes.

How many times do you think I heard, during the recession, sentiments such as, "I can't grow my business, there's a recession going on", or, "The banks aren't lending money". Even some of the employees who worked for banks at the time were saying, "Business owners don't want to borrow money"!

In 2008, if we look at the overall GDP growth for the UK (Source: Office for National Statistics), we were *minus a bit*. We went from +2.5% in 2007 to -0.3% in 2008 and -4.2% in 2009. In 2010, we were running at +1.7% and we have been positive right up until the impact of COVID-19. And, one thing is for sure, it will be positive again.

But, here's the point. Even during those two years of negative economic growth, there were businesses growing, and businesses going bust in *every single sector*. Life didn't come to a standstill.

Fact.

During the period from 2010 to early 2020, we were *plus a bit* in terms of growth, i.e. the economy has been growing consistently in that period. Also, in the same way, there were businesses growing and going bust in every sector.

Another fact.

What does this tell you?

The recession was an excuse. Sure, it was tough. I had challenging times in my business. I haemorrhaged cash and got some pretty interesting business lessons in that time. People told me that "people don't need a coach in a recession" and that "coaching is a discretionary spend, so of course it will be cut". I'm ashamed to say that, as things became more painful, and I started to look for ways out, I believed them for a while.

Not only did I choose to stop being accountable and responsible for my business, I started to blame the economy for my position. I even blamed my franchise for a period of time. Then I started to collude with the excuses of people not needing a coach. And, finally, I just descended into complete denial and used the fact that I was training for a marathon and running 70 miles per week as an excuse to not do anything about it and hope that it would go away.

But, when I look back, here are the facts:

- I kept existing clients.
- I attracted new clients.
- But not enough of them.

What was the reason for that?

My marketing wasn't good enough to get to the people who needed my help.

And that's it. The only reason. It was the truth being hidden by the list of excuses.

If I'd have understood this, I would have been one of the businesses in my sector (and there were plenty) who were growing.

What will the next excuse be? Because one thing I am certain of: there will *always* be one (or many).

I'm not saying that these situations aren't serious or won't have an impact. But the reality is this: whatever happens will happen and we can't control that. What we can control is how we approach what is happening. And if we approach events with an above the line mindset, we'll definitely get a better result.

Back to the First Test

Before we go any further, take your piece of paper from the performance model exercise, and look back at the interference you wrote down; the thing that was causing you to lower your score.

Now make a judgement: is what you wrote down above or below the line of choice, in your opinion?

If you're like 98% of people who've done this exercise with me (and we're talking thousands), then you'll have written down something that's below the line; in other words, your chances of achieving a 10 are precisely *zero*.

If you've got something that's above the line, congratulations. You're on your way to high-performance decision-making and better results.

If you're going to have a high-performing business, how many people in that business need to know this concept?

All of them!

How much blame, excuse and denial are you seeing in yourself and your business right now?

Though this is a seemingly simple concept to understand, it goes much deeper than on first inspection. Let me give you an example to illustrate this.

I have already mentioned that our results are an effect of our thoughts. Doesn't it stand to reason therefore, that if we want to change our results, we must first change our thoughts?

But, to change our actions, we need to take *ownership* (above the line) of our thoughts, don't we? This also seems obvious. But here's where the subtlety kicks in.

You see, our language represents our thoughts, so our language needs to be right. Let me explain. When we talk about ourselves, and we like what we are talking about, we tend to start the sentence with the word "I". ("I'm really good at…") We take full ownership of that thought, represented by the use of "I".

However, when we talk about ourselves, and it's an aspect of our performance that we're not so keen on, our subconscious mind cleverly shifts the language for most people: "You know how it is when you have kids. You're just so busy that there's no time to…"

How much ownership can you hear in *that* language?

If there's no ownership of the language (and therefore the thought), we won't examine it to see how we can perform better. In our perception, at that point in time, everything that's happening is external to us. What, then, are the chances of changing when we choose to externalise the language to describe our behaviour?

I spend varying amounts of time correcting clients on their language patterns, as it's only when they take ownership of their thoughts that they take ownership of the associated actions to change their performance.

How often do you notice this change in language pattern going on in yourself and your team?

Obviously, we can't be above the line all the time (and if we think we can, we're already in denial.)

But we need to choose that option more of the time if we are going to have the life and business we want. The key is remembering that, when we choose below the line, this is an effect or outcome of something. And there's always a cause.

Therefore, if we're going to truly understand how to be above the line more of the time (potential), then we need to recognise our, and our team's, current behaviour (performance), identify the things getting in the way (interference), and eliminate them as far as possible.

What impact could it have if you taught this concept to the team, and made it part of the common language in your business?

What's Holding you Back? The Power of Stubbornness and Fear

Believe it or not, there are only a few things which cause us to choose below the line. Of course, there are lots of reasons, but when we look at the categories that such reasons fall into, there are, in fact, only two.

Who knew that moving to above the line, most of the time, could be so easy!

Come up with any below the line thinking (for example, "there's not enough time…") and the cause of that statement will fall into one of two headings: stubbornness or fear.

Stubbornness: The "I Know" Attitude

How many times do you think I have heard: "That won't work in my business"? There's an obvious question in response: When was the last time you tried? And guess what the answer frequently comes back as? Of course, this attitude will stop anyone from trying anything new, and will always be powered by blame, an excuse, or blatant denial. Frequently I hear such statements as: "We've tried marketing and it didn't work for us", or, "There's no loyalty in this game", or, "Our business is different because…" These are all great examples of what we call sweeping generalisations. The thought is, for example, that because one type of marketing has been tried and didn't work, it can't ever work. As a result, marketing is now ruled out as a waste of time and money, and one crucial aspect of building the business is ignored.

It's really important to keep an open mind and try new things or new approaches to existing things. Otherwise, how can you possibly know that something won't work? Even when you have tried it, the fact that it didn't work as expected the first time isn't a good enough reason to stop. Just imagine if, when we were learning to drive, we failed our test the first time and, as a result, formed the opinion: "I can't drive". Instead, most of us chose a different response: I need to pass my test to give me the freedom to go on the journeys I really want to go on (sounds like a business doesn't it?). It's the same in business. What are the chances of being good at *anything* the first time we try it? In fact, at one point in time, you weren't even good at the thing that you started your business doing.

Remember that, for any given situation, everyone will have an opinion. Everyone's opinion is right for them at that point in time, because it's based on their current knowledge and beliefs. Any change in this knowledge or set of beliefs may prompt new questions, leading to different decisions, actions and results. We have to be open-minded, and accepting of other people's opinions, otherwise there's no opportunity for new knowledge. Go back to my statement at the beginning of this book: the thoughts I am sharing with you are based on my current knowledge, and I don't expect you to agree with them all. All I do ask is that you remain open to considering them. My knowledge is not (nor will it ever be) the finished article, and I would suggest yours will never be either. Unless, of course, you choose "I know". In which case, don't expect too many changes in your results.

This "I know" attitude is very simple to understand but, like all of the principles we are talking about, it goes much deeper.

How many times have you noticed that the person with whom you're speaking is waiting for the full stop (or maybe even the comma) in your sentence so that they can give you their opinion?

What's that really saying to you (albeit maybe only at a subconscious level)? Is it that your opinion is not valid? Over time, this may mean that your willingness to offer that opinion will diminish.

How much does this happen in your business right now? If we are teaching our teams that *our* opinion is the *only* valid opinion, then we are teaching them to stop thinking for themselves, as there's no point in them wasting energy when their opinion isn't accepted. Over time, trust will start to erode between you all as they don't feel valued and you don't value them. It's not possible to do less *and* achieve freedom from your business with that strategy.

Consider this as an alternative: what are the chances, should we have enough respect to truly understand and consider others' opinions, that we may synergise? What do I mean by that? The whole can become greater than the sum of the parts; or, indeed, a completely new and better idea can be borne out of two or more independent ideas.

Ban the words "I know" from your vocabulary. Instead, replace them with: "Isn't that interesting?" That phrase alone leaves your mind open to new possibilities, and thus increases your opportunities to change your results.

Think about the interference or "blockers" you are experiencing right now; the things which are preventing you from setting new and higher goals, or the things which you perceive are stopping you from achieving your current goals. You may be thinking: "I can't do that because…", or, "That's not possible…", or even, "That won't work…"

These are beliefs which may be holding you back from progressing towards the business you really want, and, chances are, they are just assumptions. In other words, things that you have either tried once which haven't worked as expected, or never tried. A great example of that is: "My team don't care about my business" or "There are no great people to hire out there".

Next, write down a more helpful belief as an alternative. How different would your business be if you focused on that idea instead? What would you be doing differently as a result?

FEAR: False Expectations Appearing Real

How many times have you let fear stop you from doing something? We've all been there. But how many times have you eventually needed to do the thing that was causing your fear, and realised that it wasn't so bad after all?

Let me take you back to my story at the beginning of the book. I told you that I was only a week away from not being able to pay my mortgage. What caused me to get there? Amongst other things, a scarcity mentality and, by that, I mean the fear that I was going to run out of money. As a result, I was too scared to go and try new things that cost money in my business, because, if they didn't work, I'd have even less. But, here's the thing: I was *always* going to have less money, because, as nice as I'm sure my bank manager is, at no point was he going to pause my mortgage until I sorted out my business.

There's a reason that we call it cash *flow*. If it doesn't flow, it either stagnates or evaporates.

It was a change of perspective that caused a change in my behaviour. It was only when I sat and thought about what I was (or more accurately wasn't) doing to fix my situation that the realisation came that it couldn't possibly change if I continued to behave in the way that I was. In business, we invest to achieve return on investment, and I was investing nothing, apart from negative energy, while watching my bank account deplete. I *had* to go and spend some money to find out what worked. The truth was, I had a pretty good idea what I needed to do, I was just too scared to do it. I'm sure if you've ever found yourself in a similar situation, you've also had a pretty good idea what action you needed to take. There's no rocket science in business!

How much time did you waste in that period between identifying the need and taking the action? What did you learn in that period?

Like Nike say, "*Just Do It!*"

When I tried new things, some of them worked, and some didn't. But, lo and behold, my business started to turn around. All the stories I'd been telling myself about running out of money could only have come true if I'd continued to feel the fear and not try new ideas. And that's why we have an acronym for FEAR:

False **E**xpectations **A**ppearing **R**eal.

What fear really means is that we have hit the edge of our comfort zone. Let's think about it in this context to get a good understanding of what's really happening.

Imagine a pan of water on a stove. It starts to heat up, and bubbles start to form. Keep applying the heat and the bubbles start to move towards the surface. At this point, there's massive energy being created in the water by the bubbles, pushing upwards towards the surface of the water. There's also pressure from the air pushing down on the surface of the water. The result is huge tension.

It takes a massive amount of continually applied heat to get the bubbles to break through and change state. Can you imagine those poor bubbles getting squashed up against the surface of the water? How uncomfortable that must be. It's because they are *right at the edge of their comfort zone,* just before they reach their transformation point*!* If they could speak, they'd be begging for the heat to be turned down.

If we are going to break through and achieve a new level of success, we have to keep the heat on, and maintain that pressure. We must get out of our comfort zone. Alternatively, we can turn down the heat and everything will go back to how it was.

Often, when we reach this point of discomfort, we allow fear to take over and we choose to turn down the heat.

However, no breakthroughs were ever made by making that

choice. In other words, it's great to recognise that you're hitting the edge of your comfort zone. You can choose to see it as negative and scary (remember what fear stands for) or accept it as the opportunity that it represents; the opportunity for growth and the opportunity to expand your comfort zone and achieve new results.

This response to fear is a natural phenomenon; we can all cite numerous examples of situations where we have needed to step outside of our comfort zone. When we reach that point, it normally means that our senses are piqued, and our natural protective instincts will kick in and look after us. Let's face it, they have until now, haven't they? How many times have you pushed through that feeling in your life already? How much discomfort did you experience when you started your business? You chose to keep the gas turned up then, in one of the biggest risks you've probably ever taken. So why would you choose to let that feeling of discomfort hold you back from growth and advancement now?

When you think about it, it's relatively simple: because we'd rather hang on to what we have got, than grow into what we could have. I urge you to consider the fact that other choices are available, and life, in the main, becomes easier and better the more often we choose to recognise and push through those points of discomfort.

Take five minutes and write down all the areas where you are feeling fear right now. It's time to be honest with yourself. By admitting those fears, you automatically move above the line of choice as long as you then address them.

It might be something as simple as going to a networking event. It could be getting rid of that team member who you know is no good for your business.

We all do this to ourselves – it's human nature. But, the really interesting question to ask yourself is: what are those fears stopping you from doing? Conversely, write down what, if you chose to put those fears aside, you would be doing differently in your business as a result.

What would the difference be between where you are now, and that place?

When you choose to succumb to fear, it prevents you from stepping into a new comfort zone. As a result, you consign yourself to doing the same thing over and over again, and it's all because we perceive that we might fail.

Fear of Failure and How it Cripples Us

Many people have an innate fear of failure, whether they realise it or not. But, of course, that depends on how you define the word, doesn't it? I ask the question regularly and am frequently met with something like: "Not hitting my goals". Is that really a failure?

Of course, nobody wants to fail. It's quite normal therefore to attach an emotion to the idea of failure: fear. But we need to examine this idea more closely.

Due to a definition that most of us were given at school, we've attached the wrong meaning to the word "failure" and the idea of not hitting our goals. Think about it; we were fed into a system at five years old that was entirely focused on a set of exams at the end. You either passed or failed. For 11 years, our social conditioning was about the importance of getting through those exams, and the dire consequences if we didn't "achieve".

No wonder so many of us are fearful. We've been brainwashed for pretty much all of our formative years. It's time to reframe the definition of that word once and for all.

What if we took those instances of "failure" as feedback and learning opportunities? How much more could we learn and grow?

Even if, at 16, we had absolutely screwed up our exams, would this really have been a "failure"? I'm sure the world would have kept turning. I'm sure that it would have been possible to sit the exams again if they had been important enough to us. I'm also sure that, some years later, it really wouldn't have mattered at all. Therefore, if we chose to frame it as such, that experience would just have taught us that we didn't know enough, or didn't work hard enough, or didn't seek the help available to us, or even that they simply weren't important enough.

Not hitting a goal isn't a failure, it's a learning or feedback opportunity, if you choose to see it as such.

There is only one true failure, and that's the failure to *try* in the first place: the failure to *participate*.

Go back to the story I told you about my business as I haemorrhaged cash back in 2010. How much do you think I was participating? The answer is, of course, not at all. I'd paralysed myself with fear and, as a result, was taking no action. The only lesson was that my inaction was making things worse; though, of course, I didn't see that at the time, as I was too busy trying to hang on to what little I had left.

Let's go full circle on this. If we choose to let fear or an "I know" attitude dominate our thinking, this will most likely cause us not to participate, or try something new. At that point, there's only one place we can go: below the line of choice.

There are huge chasms in most businesses where participation isn't happening. By that I mean the stuff that really needs to be done being done.

In many, that would be management, creating the systems to run the business, or planning, for example. In other words, all the things that will change the current reality into a new one. That's the effect.

The cause is: "That won't work in my business", or, "It's just easier and quicker if I do it myself" (otherwise known as the "I know" attitude), or, "I don't know how to" (otherwise known as fear). But, really, in the cold light of day, they're all just borne out of a below the line approach to thinking.

Self-Sabotage: Setting Safe Goals that Undermine our Potential

In short, our desire to stay the same (because same is safe) often limits our thinking or causes us to hold on to our old ideas and fight to protect them. Wouldn't you agree? But this doesn't change our results.

In every aspect of our lives, we operate within a current set of beliefs (we'll cover this later) about what is and is not possible. As a result, we limit our thinking, because what we *believe* is possible, and what actually *is* possible, are normally two entirely different things. In business, this can cause us to set smaller, safer goals rather than think big. But, if we think small, how *differently* do we need to think?

For example, to improve our performance by 10%, it's probably possible to work 10% harder. But what if we thought about doubling our performance? The likelihood is that it wouldn't be possible to work twice as hard (why would we?) so we tend not to set the goal in the first place!

In reality, therefore, many of us set "safe" goals, which sit within what we currently believe is possible. Because we then might only need to work harder rather than think differently, it's possible that we miss out on achieving them and, as a result, replay our previous performance. In other words, we sabotage what *could* be for what we believe *can* be, and how *"I know"* is that?

I've seen this happen many times in business owners that I work with. The point is this: is it possible to double performance without working twice as hard? Of course. We just don't know how, so we don't set the goal. But that's the thing that many people just don't realise about goals. If you know how to do it, it's not a goal, it's a task and you should just get on with it. A goal is something which requires different thought leading to different action. We have to grow into our goals. More on that later too.

SUMMARY

We've covered the barriers to thinking smarter in this chapter. It is, of course, perfectly natural to want to protect the way that we see the world. By this, I mean that we have created a story for ourselves about our place in the world and what we perceive to be possible and what's not. We all need to know where we stand, as it gives us stability and it forms the foundations of our comfort zone. All of that is fine, as long as you are where you want to be in your life and business as a result of that story. Few people are.

If you're not, then we have identified, in this chapter, some valuable strategies and explanations around what's holding you back. We all experience fear in our lives; we all have an "I know" attitude to certain things; we all choose not to try certain things as a result. That means we can all drop below that line of choice sometimes.

As a result of what you've learned so far, you should now be able to recognise the areas of your life where you are choosing to respond in an above the line of choice way, and those areas where you're below the line of choice. You will also be able to identify whether it's fear or "I know" which are the cause of your choices. You'll recognise the areas where you are choosing not to participate (or try), which will of course cause your results to stay largely the same. You'll also be able to see the effect that these choices have on the goals that you choose to set.

By accepting that these principles apply to every decision or action that every human makes, you're now in a position to understand it, and therefore change it. You have the tools to start thinking smarter.

Chapter 2

The Blueprint for Thinking Smarter

INTRODUCTION

In the last chapter we identified the principles which will help you to start thinking smarter and recognise some of the barriers which will inevitably be holding you back.

Now that you're starting to think differently, we need to consider some ideas which will help you move from where you are currently to a different place, one of life and business freedom. As we go through these ideas, I urge you to remember what you learned in Chapter 1, as the potential for you to self-sabotage will be high as we go through these exercises. Why?

Because I'm going to get you to think outside of your comfort zone. To think about what you *really* want your life to be like. And it will be easy to draw a negative conclusion very quickly: "That's just not possible for me". In that very thought appears the "I know" attitude which will stop you setting bigger goals because you believe that you may not achieve them (fear). Remember, there can only be one result here: below the line of choice thinking. Beware!

If we are going to think about really changing our results, then we need to remove the constraints from our thinking. We need the success formula (see figure 2.1).

The Success Formula

Ultimately, all of us want to become more successful in some aspect of our lives. It's really interesting, however, that the number of people who have actually *defined* what success means for them is relatively low.

In real terms, success means achieving a desired outcome, wouldn't you agree? This may take time and persistence but, unless we are clear on what that outcome is, we are highly unlikely to get there.

It makes sense, therefore, that if we're considering success as the achievement of our set outcomes, then we should start by defining clearly what those outcomes should be.

As a result of this, the success formula begins with us considering our dreams.

Here's the formula:

Dream
X
Goal
X
Learn
X
Plan
X
Action
=
SUCCESS

Figure 2.1: The success formula

We need to examine this formula closely. If you look carefully at it, you'll notice that it's a compounding equation. What I mean by that is that the results of each stage have an impact on the overall result. First question: on a scale of 1 to 10, how would you rate the quality of your dreams right now? If you've scored low, then think about the impact of that on the result of the formula! (By the way, if you haven't got any dreams, then it's a zero, and zero times anything is *zero*!)

Defining your Dreams

If the quality of our dreams is low, then the quality of our goals can only ever be low; hence, not much will change.

I'm going to encourage you to dream BIG! What would you do if money or time were not an object for consideration?

Let your imagination run wild. If your dreams scare you, good! If a little voice in your head springs up and screams, "That's not possible" (or some derivation thereof), then I'll refer you to my previous points about self-sabotage, failure, fear and below the line thinking. I encourage you to stick with your dreams.

They're your dreams, and the people who criticise them will be going through fear or self-sabotage too. That's their problem and your dreams are, quite frankly, none of their business. What are the constraints on dreams? None!

> *"So many of our dreams at first seem impossible, then they seem improbable, and then, when we summon the will, they soon become inevitable."*
> – Christopher Reeve

Has someone else done it (or something similar) before you? Then it's possible. All you have to do is find out *how* (hence the "learn" in the equation).

If your dreams *are* of good quality, chances are that you're going to need to set some stretching goals. Wouldn't that be fair to say?

So, it's time to get some big dreams. Let's give you some tools to firstly define your dreams, and then embed them firmly in your mind in order that your very clever subconscious starts to find ways to manifest them for you.

Set aside some quality time to do this exercise. It's fun to do with your whole family.

Creating Your Dreamboard

Get a very large piece of paper; perhaps some wallpaper or a piece of flipchart paper. Now, sit down and start to create a list of all the things you want to have and do. That may be big things like houses and cars, or smaller things like holidays and experiences. Find a representative picture of each thing, either in a magazine or on the internet, and stick it on to your big piece of paper. Let your imagination run wild. Why wouldn't you? After all, these are your *dreams*, and we've already agreed that you're not allowed to self-sabotage. You only have to put the things you want to do and have on there right now. You can figure out how you're going to make them happen later. Remember the order of the success formula.

When you finish, you'll have a huge visual representation of everything that you and your family want to experience. We'll call it your dreamboard. You should put this somewhere very prominent to continuously remind you of your dreams. Now, if this doesn't achieve two things, I would be *very* surprised.

First, it should get you really excited! Imagine yourself ticking off all those things and either owning or doing the things in your pictures.

Second, it should start to get you thinking differently about your life. You can pretty much budget out your dreamboard (only roughly of course) and, when you add up the costs, I guarantee that you'll have to start thinking about a different business to facilitate it for you; most probably a different level of earnings *and* the ability to leave your business for longer periods of time to allow you the freedom to accomplish these things.

By the way, what happens when you have achieved all those things on your dreamboard?

Make a new one of course.

Setting Goals: The Roadmap to Your Dreams

OK, so now we've got a visual representation of all those exciting things which almost definitely requires a business which can afford you the freedom to do them. So, we're going to need to set some different business goals, aren't we?

It's vitally important to refer to those previous principles and the success formula here. When we set goals, they're obviously the roadmap to achieving our dreams. But, even though the destination may be clear, the route isn't always quite so obvious. It's *okay* to set goals which you don't yet know how to achieve and in fact, I'd positively encourage it.

Why do I say that? Because, if our goals don't cause us both fear and excitement, then they're probably not goals, just tasks that we need to get on with. If that's the case, then I'd suggest that you revisit your dreamboard and think about what your goals *really* need to be to give you *that* life!

By the way, it's worth mentioning something here as we consider goals. While I understand that there are going to be short and medium-term goals for your business and life, there should be an overarching business goal: when will your business be finished?

What do I mean by that?

Let's think for the moment about the definition of a business. When I ask new clients or seminar attendees how they define it, I usually get such ideas as, "Something that makes money", or, "An entity that exchanges goods or services for money." Those ideas are all correct, with one major omission.

Let me explain.

I assume that there will come a time when you'll need to exit your business, unless you're planning to live forever (in which case sell that secret and you'll make a fortune!) To exit, it will need to operate without needing you to be there, won't it? If it doesn't operate without you, your options become more limited – give it away or close it. If it does, it can be sold or continue to pay you an income when you're not there.

And, presumably, if you plan to sell your business at some point in the future, you'll want to get a great return on your investment of money, time, energy and emotion?

Let's think about this book for a moment. Say I'd written the title and then listed out the chapter headings, but that's it, nothing more. I knew what the content would be, but it just remained in my head. How much would you have paid for the book?

Nothing! And I wouldn't blame you. What's the book worth now that it's written? It must be worth something if you're still reading it!

Why would your business be any different? If you're holding all the keys to your business in your head, and you're inextricably linked to it so that it can't run effectively without you, how much is that business worth? How easy is it to exit without causing substantial damage to its performance?

That's why so many business owners get to the end of their working life and just close their businesses, or hand them over for no return. What a shame.

ActionCOACH's definition of a real business is this:

"A commercial, profitable enterprise that works without YOU"

When will you have one of those? Isn't that the first goal you should write down? After all, there's an inevitability around time passing and you ending up at the point where you have to do *something* with your business. Why not have it ready for sale? If you're not thinking about that, then we may as well call it denial (below the line thinking). Because, as sure as eggs is eggs, it's going to happen at some point.

Why not start thinking about it now? Stephen R. Covey in his book, *The 7 Habits of Highly Effective People*, documents his second habit as: "Start with the end in mind". Meaning that we should always consider the final destination first before planning the route.

Imagine getting in your car in Birmingham, driving north on the M6 towards Stoke and, half an hour into your journey, you realise that you actually wanted to get to London. Whenever we go on a journey in our car, we know *precisely* where we are going. If we didn't, it would not only be a frustrating trip, but we wouldn't know if we were on track. Sometimes we need to make a diversion because of an accident or a traffic jam, but the satnav always reroutes us to the final destination, doesn't it?

It's the same principle for our business. We're all going on a business journey. What's your destination? Chances are, if you haven't defined it yet, you're going around in circles. Imagine doing that in your car.

That's why, when many business owners I meet tell me that they have 20 years' experience in their business, I will often ask if they *really* have 20 years of experience, or one year repeated 20 times.

By the way, do make sure the way you frame your goals focuses on what you *do* want, not what you *don't* want. Try typing in to Google "not Christmas trees". What are the results? Pictures of Christmas trees, and links to Christmas tree review and shopping sites.

In the same way that Google doesn't notice the "not" in your search, nor does our brain; so, "I don't want to run out of money" isn't a great goal!

Goals are designed to serve three purposes:

1. To create direction and focus
2. To create movement and momentum
3. To provide the direction for personal growth

Let's look briefly at each of those in turn:

1. To create direction and focus.

There's a part of our brain called our Reticular Activating System (RAS). Without being overly scientific about this, it's the part which helps us filter out information so that we achieve or find evidence of what we focus on. When we write down our goals, it sets our RAS, and our brain begins to look (even subconsciously) for ways to achieve them. In the absence of clear goals, what is our brain focused on finding? More of the same, because we haven't told it to look for anything else! Hence, the second reason for setting goals.

2. To create movement and momentum

Your goals, as we've already stated are at a point which is different to where you are right now. As such, you need to move to achieve them, whether that be physically or by changing your thoughts and actions.

They're your focus and should inspire you to keep moving towards them.

Why did I choose the word *inspire*, do you think?

Let me explain.

Many people talk about being motivated: one more big *push*. Sounds like hard work, doesn't it? In my opinion, motivation is the lesser driver because it can be applied externally. This book, for example, should motivate you to go and think differently and take some new action. Yet that motivation may not last. It may become tough, and you may decide to go back to the way it was because that was easier. Motivation is also therefore a transient force: it comes and goes. We can't rely on it to get us to our destination because it's not always there to push us.

Inspiration, on the other hand, is most definitely an internal force. When we're inspired, we are *pulled* towards something with conviction. It's a more permanent force as we are excited by the outcome. If you've done the exercise with your dreamboard, chances are that you're feeling pretty inspired, right? If you haven't done the exercise, stop! Do it now, because the inspiration that it will awaken in you will be your driving force and guiding light when times get tough.

3. To provide the direction for personal growth

For me, this is the most exciting aspect and we'll delve deeper into this idea in a moment. I've already suggested that if you want to change the outputs, you're going to have to change the inputs. In other words, you'll need to change the way you think, and ask better quality questions, if you're going to take better decisions and get better results.

I've already said that, when we set goals, they should scare us. We shouldn't be entirely sure how we'll achieve them because they push us out of our comfort zone. There's a well-known acronym to do with goals which is widely used: SMART, which stands for:

S – Specific

The goal must give you a very clear picture of what the outcome is.

M – Measurable

There should be an objective way to determine if the goal has been achieved.

A – Achievable

The goal should be achievable.

R – Relevant
The goal should be relevant to you.

T -Timely
The goal should have a timescale attached to it.

Personally, I'm not a fan of this acronym. The goals I'm encouraging you to set, which push you beyond what you might currently believe is achievable, would fail the SMART criteria and, as a result, we might lower our goals to a level we consider more feasible. In other words, we would end up setting goals which are *inside* our comfort zone. Here we are back at self-sabotage, fear, failure to participate, and, ultimately, dipping below that line of choice, blaming, making excuses or in denial.

Moreover, when we lower the goal to something which sits within our current paradigm (i.e. what we believe is possible), and we don't quite achieve it, then we fall *really* short of where we need to be to achieve the business and the life we want.

If our goals are scary yet exciting, and we only achieve 80%, for example, so what! Chances are that we will still have achieved more than we originally thought possible. We will have moved towards our dreams faster, *and* we will have absorbed some new learning on the way to help us accelerate our results going forward.

By the way, goals *must* be written down. If we hold them in our head, they're an idea, not a goal. I'm sure you'll agree that the ideas you hold in your head often "move to the right". By that I mean they often don't quite come to pass in the originally intended timescale.

Write down your goals now.

The first goal should be the date that your business will be finished.

Next, if that date is more than five years away, write down your five-year goals, then your three-year goals. These are milestones, nothing more. When you're driving down the motorway at speed, you only need to know that you're heading in the right direction and are going to reach your ultimate destination at roughly the time you planned. You've probably got a stop planned, and you know roughly what time you should get to a specific point in your journey. You can't see the services yet though.

Now write down your one-year goals. These should be clearer, as you're not looking quite so far into the distance. If we continue to use the motorway analogy, this might be the next junction. Perhaps you can't quite see it yet, but you know precisely where it is.

Now write down your 90-day goals. This is the next motorway bridge you can see in the distance. You still have to drive a while to reach it, but it's visible. Which lane do you choose? This is tactical planning, and we'll cover that later.

Just a reminder: remember to write down your personal goals as well as your business goals. We're looking to achieve a great business *and* a great life, aren't we?

Now that we have some clear goals, it's time to consider that third point: the person we need to become to achieve them.

Becoming the Person Who Can Achieve Their Dreams

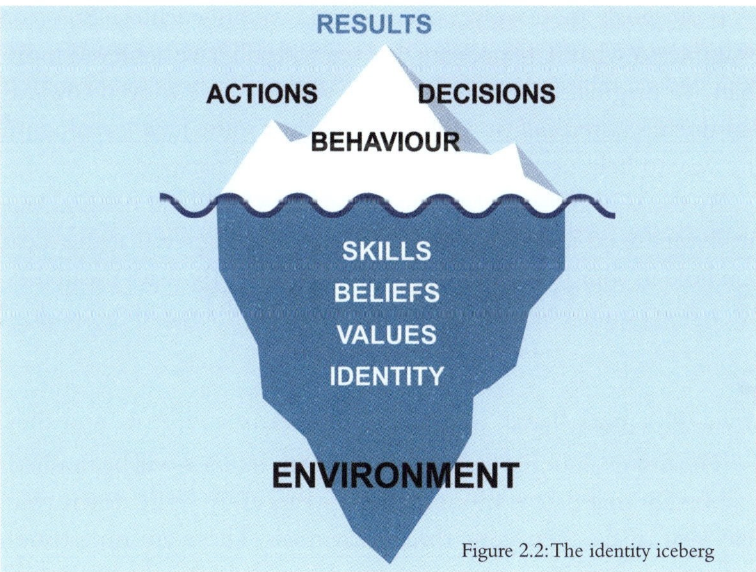

Figure 2.2: The identity iceberg

This is one of the most powerful diagrams you will ever see. That's a pretty dramatic statement, isn't it?

Let's get some definitions clear first.

Results – the outcome of our actions.

Behaviour – the things we do, demonstrated by the decisions we make and the actions we take.

Skills – the things we're good at.

Beliefs – things that we hold to be true at a point in time. How quickly can we change a belief? Instantly! We've changed our beliefs all through our lives. Remember when you believed in Santa Claus, and then someone told you he didn't exist? (Apologies if that just ruined Christmas for you!)

Values – things that we hold to be important. They're less changeable, though big life events like getting married or having children may cause some shifts. Values are things like fairness, integrity, etc.

Identity – let's just say that this is our subconscious mind. It's designed to reinforce who we think we are – more on that in a moment.

Now the definitions are out of the way, let's relate the iceberg to a formula: the formula for life success.

BE x DO = HAVE

Figure 2.3: The formula for life success

If we start from "have", these are our dreams and goals, and they equate to the "results" level of the iceberg (figure 2.2).

Our behaviour, i.e. our actions and decisions, cause our results: that's the "do".

Notice how the portion of the iceberg above the waterline (behaviour) represents only a small percentage of the overall structure. So, when we're considering new results, we need new behaviour, but we're going to need to dig deeper to cause that to happen.

What causes our behaviour? Everything below the waterline on the iceberg: that's "be". Largely though, our beliefs drive our behaviour, and our behaviour reinforces our beliefs. Finally, our subconscious mind finds evidence of our beliefs to reinforce who we believe ourselves to be.

If you want a different result, you need to take different action. This probably means that you'll need to learn something new or improve a skill; you'll also maybe need to develop a new belief. Back to the principles we covered a while ago. If you believe that something won't work (and that's the "I know" attitude creeping in, by the way), then you'll never behave in that way.

Our subconscious looks to reinforce our beliefs. Let me give you an example: let's say you think you're terrible at football. You're kicking a ball around (though this may even be unlikely, because why would you do something which you're no good at?) Yet you score a goal! Your subconscious mind, as it believes that you are terrible at football, registers this as a fluke! Conversely, when you kick the ball and it goes flying off in the wrong direction, your subconscious mind tells you: "Told you you're terrible".

This means it's really important to examine our beliefs when we set a goal. Unless we change our beliefs, the likelihood of achieving our goal is… zero!

Let's look at beliefs more closely.

Bricks or Rubble?

When I teach the concept of the iceberg to clients, I talk about "the bag of bricks". The bag of bricks are the beliefs we carry round with us. For the most part, we never really stop and examine them. Some of them don't even belong to us; they were perhaps given to us by a parent or friend, e.g. "Money doesn't buy happiness.", and we accepted them without consideration, popped them in our bag (the belief system), carried them around with us and found evidence to reinforce them again and again.

Our subconscious doesn't know whether our beliefs are helpful or unhelpful. It's designed only to find more and more evidence of our beliefs in order to show us that they're true. That's it.

Our beliefs have helped us get to where we are right now. In that respect, we can call them bricks. After all, bricks give us a solid structure. Our current "be" (our skill set and belief system) causes our current "do" (actions and behaviours), which in turn causes our current "have" (level of results).

Consider this, however: when we set a goal (which by its definition is a place removed from where we are right now – a new "have"), then we're going to need to take different actions ("do"). Chances are, therefore, that we may need to change some beliefs as we've already agreed that our beliefs cause our behaviour ("be"). Our current bricks, therefore, aren't so useful anymore (because they only provide a solid foundation for where we are right now), and, consequently, they become rubble when we consider the results we want to achieve. You can't build with rubble, can you?

What I'm really saying is that sustainable changes in behaviour aren't possible unless we change our beliefs first or start to look for new evidence in order to form new beliefs. If we don't change our beliefs, then our subconscious continues to look for evidence of the old beliefs, reinforces them, and anchors us to our old behaviours.

> *"Man often becomes what he believes himself to be. If I keep on saying to myself that I cannot do a certain thing, it is possible that I may end by really becoming incapable of doing it. On the contrary, if I shall have the belief that I can do it, I shall surely acquire the capacity to do it, even if I may not have it at the beginning."* ~ Mahatma Gandhi

Let me give you an example. It's not unusual for a technician to start a business. If, for example, an electrician takes the risk of starting his own venture, he must believe that he is exceptional within his craft – perhaps the best in the business.

That's great when he's self-employed, working as a one-man band. The challenge arises when he starts employing people. If his belief remains that he's the best electrician, who do you think is going to be the busiest person in the business? At every opportunity, he'll put his cape on, slip his underpants over his trousers, and engage Superman mode! He'll continuously step in to save the day, and his subconscious will reinforce that he is, as expected, the best man for the job. The pattern remains unbroken!

But, who's left running the business while Superman is off saving the day? Unless said electrician changes his belief system around his and others' capabilities, he'll not move into the position of business owner (even though his title says otherwise). He'll remain permanently busy working *in* the business, not *on* it.

As such, if we're going to change our results and move towards our goals, then we need to reprogramme our subconscious to find new evidence of more helpful beliefs, or bricks, which we can then build on. We can do that systematically using what we call affirmations. The concept of affirmations has been popular throughout history. More recently, Napoleon Hill called it "auto-suggestion" in *Think and Grow Rich*[3], and you'll see the idea crop up in many of the books on self-development and success.

We actually do it informally all the time anyway, so we already know it works! The challenge is that the majority of us are doing it in an unsystematic way, and without consideration of whether what we're telling ourselves is helping us move forwards or not. Let me give you an example. How many times have you said to yourself, "I am having a bad day", in the morning, and subsequently everything that has happened that day has led you to reinforce that perception? Our mind is only there to follow instructions so, if you've set up a belief that you're having a bad day, you've given the instruction to your subconscious to find more and more evidence of that belief so you can prove yourself correct.

What if you'd chosen a different statement? What if you'd said, "I'm having a bad half hour"? That provides room for your subconscious to believe that there's hope for the rest of the day.

If you look at the construction of the statement, "I am having a

[3] Napoleon Hill, "Think and Grow Rich", Vermilion; Rev Ed edition (7 Oct. 2004)

bad day", it begins with an identity level statement: I am. There is complete ownership of that statement. Our subconscious only ever wants to reinforce the perception of what we believe to be true, so it will take all of the good things that happen during the bad day and ignore them, simply because it's not looking for evidence of a *good* day.

The reality is, we're telling ourselves all kinds of things all the time, some of which may be helpful, some not. Chances are, we can find evidence of anything we choose to, because we all know that we get what we focus on. Let's go back to our previous example of "I'm a terrible footballer". There's a good chance that, when we're kicking a ball around, there's going to be some examples of some bad shots, some mediocre shots and even some good ones. If our subconscious is only looking to reinforce the current belief, it takes all the evidence of mediocre and good, and puts it to one side, as this doesn't align. The evidence is there, we just need to notice it to change our perception of ourselves.

If we can influence our subconscious that easily, why wouldn't we want to do it in a systematic way to help us move more quickly and effectively towards our goals and dreams?

Creating an Identity Shift

If we want to change our results (our "have"), then we need to change our behaviour (our "do"). We'll only change that sustainably if we get rid of the rubble (the beliefs which are keeping us where we are) and replace them with new bricks (fresh, more helpful beliefs, aligned to our goals). We need to systematically change our "be". Here's how.

I find it easier to do this exercise diagrammatically as it helps to visualise it.

1. First, consider the categories in your life. By that, I mean the top-level areas of your life. I think there are three, and I've not managed to find anyone who can give me anything different. They are family, business and me. I tend to draw three interlocking circles of the same size and mark each one as a category:

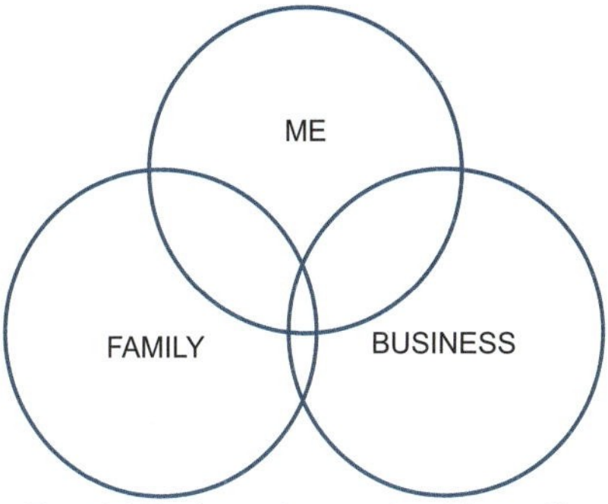

Figure 2.4: The three major categories within your life

The reason that I draw them as interlocking circles is that, if they are the three key major categories in our lives, we need to focus on keeping them balanced with one another. What I mean by that is, we shouldn't just focus on improving our capabilities in business. After all, we're looking to get more from our business *and* our life, so we should aim to improve all aspects of our lives.

2. Now, consider your roles in each of those categories. For example, in the family category, my roles are husband, father to Oliver and father to Alex. The reason I've separated out the father roles is because they both need different things; more on that soon. In the business category, I'm an MD, a salesperson, a coach and a presenter. In the me category, we divide it into the subcategories that keep us healthy and happy. I've got health, wealth, friends and community.

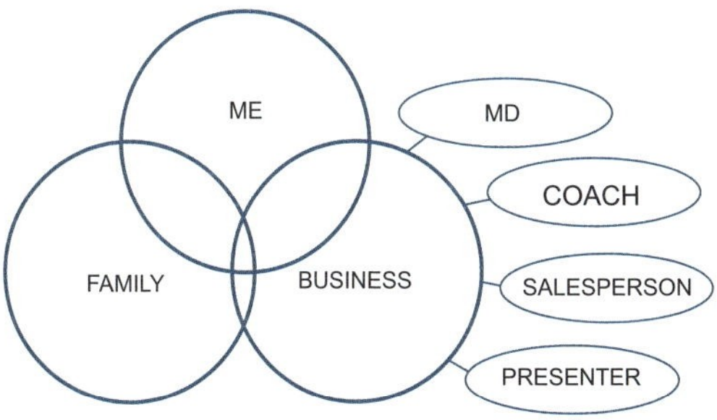

Figure 2.5: Roles within the business category

3. When you've defined your roles or subcategories, think of the goals for each one. What do you want to achieve to help you move towards your overarching goals in your business and your life?

   To give you an example, take my salesperson role (see figure 2.5). My goal in this role is:

   "To ensure that everyone I meet is well enough informed to make an educated decision on whether coaching is the right vehicle for them to achieve their life and business goals and convert 100% of the meetings I sit".

4. Next, consider how you'd need to behave to fulfil that goal; in other words, who would you need to be? You should be able to create a list of adjectives to describe that person.

   To continue with the salesperson example from figure 2.5, these are the words I came up with:

   - Understanding
   - Strong
   - Informative
   - Unwilling to accept excuses
   - Sincere
   - Interested
   - Helpful

5. Once you're clear on these details, write down the appropriate affirmation using the adjectives you have listed. They must all start with the words "I am" since we need our subconscious to take ownership of the statement and start to look for evidence to reinforce it.

   When you read your affirmations, they won't feel comfortable; Your subconscious may not have found evidence of you being that person, *yet*!

Here's my salesperson affirmation:

> "I am an understanding and sincere salesman and am genuinely interested in finding out what is important to people. I am strong in my belief that I can help any business and am unwilling to accept excuses or lack of self-belief when I know that I can help a potential client to achieve their goals and dreams. I am persistent in my efforts to help them buy my services and, as such, will continue to educate them until they can make a well-informed decision".

You should allow some quality time for this. It will take some thought and, like anything worth doing, you'll find that the first time you attempt this exercise, it may be quite difficult.

That's OK. These affirmations don't have to be works of art right now; they don't need to be long or perfectly written. They just need to be good enough to cause your subconscious to start to look for new evidence (a new brick).

As long as they create a shift from who you are right now towards the person you need to become to achieve your goals, then you're on the right track. Remember that you'll be rewriting these when you become that person anyway, so you're going to get much more practice.

When you have your list of affirmations, put them somewhere you will be able to access them easily. You need to read them to yourself aloud.

Personally, I found that I wasn't very good at keeping that piece of paper with me. As a result, I took my iPhone, and read my affirmations into the voice recorder. Now I have them with me wherever I go and, as soon as I get into my car, I can listen to them.

Invest 10 minutes, twice a day, reading or listening to this list of affirmations out loud. This will, over time, systematically reprogramme your subconscious to find evidence of this new belief and reinforce your perception of being that person. You'll start to notice the behaviours that show you evidence of being that person; they will not only become your new comfort zone, but they will also be sustainable.

Guess what? It's then time to write a new set of affirmations.

Let me give you an example of what I mean. When I first started my coaching practice, the idea of standing in front of a room of people and presenting didn't fill me with too much excitement (and that's an understatement). I needed to become a confident presenter. As a result, one of my first affirmations was: "I am a confident presenter". And that was enough. All I needed was something which overrode my current subconscious programming of: "Oh my God, not presenting. I will definitely make a mess of that", to: "I'm OK at this".

Of course, the first time I stood up in front of a room of people, I didn't find too much evidence of being confident. The next time was a bit better, though of course there was plenty of room for improvement. The point is, my subconscious was looking for evidence of confidence, not mess ups. Soon, I became that confident presenter; my belief system changed and my behaviour (of giving good presentations) then reinforced my belief. I was then ready for the next step. Now, my affirmation is:

"I am a world-class, engaging, energetic and inspirational presenter, captivating and inspiring those who hear me speak to go and take action and have the courage and resolution to build their businesses. I am sincere and convincing in the stories I share to help potential clients make the decision to invest in coaching."

How many people have told me that I *am* now a world-class presenter? Many! I have become that person. That's quite a journey from being uncomfortable standing in front of a few people, isn't it?

I've had plenty of clients push back quite hard on the idea of affirmations. The interesting thing is, if you don't try it, how do you know if it works or not? The people who have pushed back hardest on these affirmations are now their biggest fans.

Our dreamboard exercise forced us to idealise what we wanted our life to look like and create a visual representation of it, which we should see every day.

The most important thing to remember is that the formula for "have" is "be" x "do" (see figure 2.3). It's no good writing an affirmation and not following through with the behaviour to back it up, as "be" x "don't do" = "don't have"!

The IVVM Process

Once we've created a dreamboard, we've got a pretty cool representation of the sorts of things we'd like to do and have. Our dreamboard is the first part of the IVVM process, the tool which we can use to really focus ourselves on the achievement of those dreams.

What is IVVM?

Idealise:

Your dreamboard is you investing the time to create a picture of the life you want to have. If you have done as I asked, you'll have let your imagination run wild, and by now you should be pretty inspired and excited.

Visualise:

It's now your job to visualise yourself leading that life. Your dreamboard will help as it's already a visual representation of all the stuff you're going to do along the way. Invest some time each day, at least 10 minutes, and see this as your opportunity to meditate and have some focused time to yourself.

Verbalise:

We now need to put our ideas out there in a verbal fashion. There's no point just thinking about something. Chances are, we're going to need to behave differently if we're going to head towards what we've just defined as our ideal life. To achieve that, we need our secret weapon: affirmations. Listen to or read out loud the affirmations you have just created; focus your attention on finding the evidence of you becoming the person that will achieve your dreams.

Materialise:

Provided that you follow this process *and* take the actions I'll share with you as we go through this book, you can materialise any of your dreams into reality.

Embrace New Learning

If we're going to change our results, we need to change our actions, don't we? Here's the thing though: how is it possible to change our actions without new learning?

When we set a goal, it should be something that we don't entirely know how to do, so learning is, of course, obligatory. Why is it so important? New learning causes new beliefs ("be") and new or improved skills ("do"). Let's go back to my previous example of "I'm a terrible footballer", and let's say that I decide that it's important for me to become better at football because I want to go and kick a ball around in the park with my kids and not embarrass them.

A great step in the right direction would be to go and get some football coaching. Probably, over a period of time, I'd start to improve my existing skills (or lack thereof) and learn new ones.

Let's imagine that I'd also written an affirmation which I had been disciplined about using while I was having football coaching. As my skills start to change, my beliefs about my capabilities would probably change too. As a result, I'll begin to ask myself new questions, for example, "I wonder if I could play for a team?"

The next step would be to make a new decision, which can only arise as a result of that new question. If the decision is "yes", I'll probably go and investigate some local teams to see which is appropriate for me (new action) and, when I join one, I'm likely to start getting new results as a footballer.

It's like dominoes. Push one (learn something new), and the rest topple: new belief causes new question causes new decision, and so on. But we have to push the first domino.

Let me ask you a question right now: when did you last have business lessons?

If you haven't, chances are that your level of knowledge hasn't changed in a directed fashion to help you achieve your goals. When your knowledge stagnates like this, it often leads to you running around like a crazy person trying to cover all the bases in your business.

We've already established that a true goal is one which you don't know how to achieve yet; by definition, learning must be involved. If we're going to plan for the goal effectively, we probably need to gain new knowledge in order to do it. There's no other option here if you want to move forward in your business at a quicker rate.

While it may appear difficult to know exactly what you need to learn, you have actually already taken the first step by defining your goals, both in the overarching sense and then by breaking them down into the goals that you used to create your affirmations.

If your goal is around improving your performance as the MD of your business, for example, it would make sense to go and learn about leadership and management, and how to create business systems. If you need to improve your sales performance, learn about sales strategies. This is directed learning.

The point is though, and I stress this with all my clients, that all learning is good learning. When you do more learning, there'll be some common trends appearing. I think of it like this: we begin with a current level of knowledge and accompanying beliefs. Let's imagine that as a circle (the solid inner circle, or the existing paradigm, in figure 2.6 below). When we read our first book about business, it's like watching someone in a cartoon getting bonked on the head! A big lump comes up, but it's not connected to anything. Read the next book, another lump appears, the next, another, and so on. However, once you've read a few books you'll start to notice that there are some common factors which transcend the individual titles and speak to the common principles of business. At this point, there's a pop, and your original circle gets bigger (the dotted circle in figure 2.6).

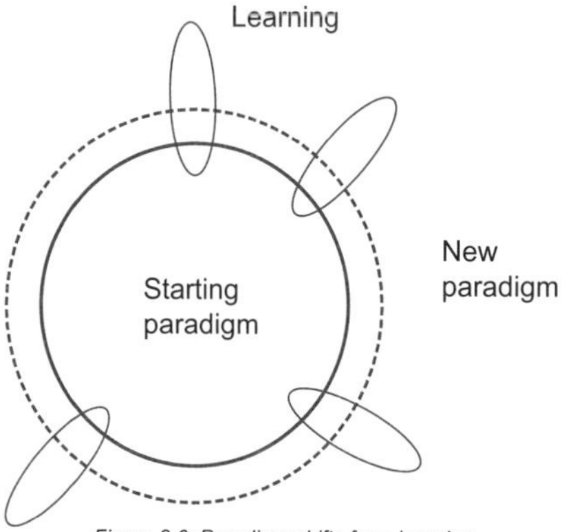

Figure 2.6: Paradigm shifts from learning

As you keep learning, you'll identify more of these common themes faster, which causes the whole pace of new learning and thoughts, and thus results to accelerate.

There is, therefore, a very simple concept to embrace when it comes to an attitude to learning, and you'll see this across much of the literature on personal development.

As Jim Rohn says, "Work harder on yourself than you do on your job".

We can also see this lesson in Brad Sugars' philosophy: "Learn before you earn. The only place where 'earn' comes before 'learn' is in the dictionary".

Write a 90-Day Plan

What does your plan look like for your business right now? And, by plan, I mean a written document with timescales and specific actions to take over the next 90 days which are aligned with your goals for your business and life.

Back to my old friend Jim Rohn, who for me sums this up best: "If you don't have a plan for your life, chances are you'll fall into someone else's plan. And guess what they've got planned for you? Not much!"

Now, I understand that quite a lot of business owners have an aversion to planning. But they are thinking back to the business plans which were required to secure funding, with made up numbers and "finger in the air" cashflows.

That's not what I am talking about here. This is most definitely an operational plan, a to-do list to achieve your goals, if you like. Each quarter, set aside at least half a day to review your last quarter's performance, define goals for the coming quarter and then write down the activities needed to make these goals happen.

Why 90 days? Because it's short enough to stay focused and long enough to achieve some real results.

Remember the analogy I used when we were goal setting. Your 90-day plan is taking you to the next bridge on the motorway. It shouldn't be too difficult to write the list of activities needed to get you there. If it is, then I refer you back to the learn section. You don't have enough knowledge yet!

When you're writing your plan, adopt a "less is more" approach. Have a maximum of three business goals for the quarter. But even one is fine. All progress is progress.

Remember, also, to plan your personal goal(s). You can't have a great business *and* a great life unless you do!

Here's the simplest way to create a plan for your next 90 days:

1. Sit and review the last 90 days in your business. Look at the areas that have gone well, and the areas which haven't quite gone as you would have liked. List them out, reflect on each one and make some notes. What did you learn? What do you need to do differently this quarter to make it work better?

2. Determine your three main goals for the coming 90 days based on this reflection, and taking consideration of your overall business goals, determined earlier. Write each goal on a Post-It note.

3. Take a packet of Post-It notes, and start to write a list of actions, one action per Post-It, until you feel that you have a good list to address each goal. Unless you have significant ability to involve your team in the execution of your plan, keep the actions to a maximum of one per week, per goal for now (maybe even less).

4. Lay out the Post-Its for each goal on a table, and then place the activity based Post-Its in a row next to the goal they relate to.

5. Reorder the Post-Its for each goal based on order of importance or any sequencing considerations.

6. Assess the list of actions for each goal, asking yourself: "If I do these actions, do I achieve this goal?" If the answer is no, add more Post-Its to ensure that you will!

7. Assign week commencing dates to each action for the coming quarter.

8. Finally, take a picture of the plan and make sure that it's permanently visible.

There you go! You don't need to do anything more complex than this. The value of the planning process is in the process itself and the thought that goes with it. No plan is perfect, but each one you write will be better than the last. It's just a question of practice. The important thing is to begin, because any plan is better than no plan.

The majority of clients I start to work with have never written an operational activity list in their business life. Few plan their day or week, never mind the next 90 days.

The rule here is to go easy on yourself and recognise that everything in your plan, no matter how simple, is designed to improve today so that it's a better tomorrow. And that's enough.

Choose to Act: The Power of Consistency and Discipline

You've done the hard work, now make it happen!

That takes discipline and, the sooner you become disciplined, the more choices you'll have. It may seem painful, but there are only two pains in life: the pain of discipline, or the pain of regret. Which will you choose?

It's the actions we take today that cause our results, so consistency is the key. I often use the "an apple a day keeps the doctor away" metaphor. If you choose an apple a day in your business, you'll be doing the tasks to keep the business healthy and move you towards your goals. And your plan provides you with those tasks, doesn't it?

Conversely, if you choose a Mars bar a day in your business, you won't see the consequences of that choice today, but it will have an impact in the long term. Let's imagine you choose the Mars bar consistently. What do you think will happen over the next few months and years? We've already talked about the business failure rate being alarmingly high. This is the result of Mars bar choices, in my opinion: poor decisions, consistently repeated. Neither success nor failure happen overnight. It is our discipline with either our good habits or our bad habits which will lead to both. And, in the main, bad habits are the result of a lack of goal clarity and knowledge which leads to poor choice of action.

You can choose to change those actions at any point. The destination is yours to reach! The question is, are you moving in the right direction right now?

SUMMARY

Here we are at our ultimate goal. Success!

It's not rocket science. Success is about doing the right things consistently. There's nothing extraordinary about it. There are only excuses for not achieving success. How many excuses do you have in your arsenal?

Of course, we have already established that, if we are going to create more success for ourselves, then we are going to have to change how we think, how we act, what we believe about ourselves, and the skills we have.

Everything is borne out of clarity. Clarity of goals and the resulting commitment to achieving your dreams will help you to succeed, even when there are obstacles placed in your way. Goal clarity is the prerequisite to planning the operational activities you'll need to undertake to achieve them, and it also forms the roadmap for the changes you'll need to make in your identity iceberg. It also determines the learning you'll need to undertake to develop your knowledge to achieve your goals. In turn then, plan and action clarity come from goal clarity; and it's the only way that success can follow.

If our final destination is life and business freedom, however, then there's one more piece of the jigsaw we need to slot into place. I have mentioned the "technician" a couple of times; the skilled person who starts a business doing what they are skilled at. Great for creating a job, but not so great for creating a business (remember, a business is defined as a commercial and profitable enterprise which can work *without* you).

This, for most, is the hardest transition to make. To forego being the best technician in the business in order to become the best business owner instead, we must climb the entrepreneurial ladder.

Chapter 3

Using Smarter Thinking to Climb the Entrepreneuarial Ladder

INTRODUCTION

The final piece of the "thinking smarter" jigsaw is the E-ladder, and it's one of my favourite coaching tools. "E" stands for entrepreneur. It also starts to form the bridge into the next section of this book: how we use our time.

Now, I realise that we might all think that we are entrepreneurs because we started our own business. But here's the thing. Entrepreneurs are right at the top of the ladder, and not many of us have made it there yet.

We'd better have a look at it and clear up some definitions.

Figure 3.1: The E-ladder

Let's start at the bottom, and not only consider the status of the person, but also their relationship with money and their mindset.

Employee

Most of us start here. Employed by someone else to perform a specific task. We exchange time for money and are guided in what we do. We *earn* money, being paid a defined consideration in exchange for a defined number of hours. Many consider that they should be earning more, failing to realise that they are not paid for their time, but for the value they bring to their time. Being an employee is the learning platform for becoming self-employed. Planned properly, a plethora of skills can be gained here using someone else's money. Few (including myself) realise this at the time, and therefore decide to start a business as a specialist, great at what they do, but with "eyes wide shut" as to what owning and running a business really entails. As an employee, our relationship with money is largely dictated by the value the marketplace puts on what we can do. There is no leverage; by which I mean that we have a defined amount of time to be exchanged for a defined amount of money.

Self-employed

At some point, if you're reading this book, I assume that you made the leap to become self-employed. It may have been a while ago, and you may now run a business with multiple team members. Importantly, self-employed isn't a position, it's a mindset.

Let's first of all consider the relationship with money. Self-employed people *make* money. They exchange hours for money, but they don't get paid unless they do. Holiday pay goes by the wayside; there's no-one else to rely on, so it's easy to just work that extra hour, isn't it?

There's also the Superman mindset we touched on earlier. Naturally, if you have the courage to step into self-employment, you need to have plenty of faith in your abilities. You have to believe that you're up there with the best at what you do. And that's fantastic, to a point.

Let me explain. I mentioned that this was a mindset, not a position. By that, I mean that there are plenty of people out there who own businesses but still have a self-employed mindset. They employ teams, yet still believe that they are the best at the operational aspects of the business which caused them to create the entity in the first place i.e. "I'm the best plumber in my business".

This normally means that they will come swooping in, shiny cape and underpants sparkling impressively in the sunlight, to "solve" all the problems in their business. Naturally, they assume they will be adored by all of their long-suffering team members for saving the day.

What's really happening here? If no-one can do it as well as you can, what are you setting yourself up for? To be tied to your business forever, exchanging time for money in relatively low-value, time-consuming operational activities? To not generating as much money when you're not there as you are the main breadwinner? To having a team who are not growing and developing because you "solve" all their problems for them. Ultimately, to having a JOB (Just Over Broke) because, with a self-employed mindset, it's simply impossible to have a business: a commercial, profitable enterprise that works *without* you.

The "be" of a self-employed person leads to the "do" of a self-employed person, and therefore the results "have" of a self-employed person.

This is why so many people build a team, only to find it doesn't work as they expected, and scale back to just themselves; they fall back into the same mindset of "no-one can do it as well as I can", and "it's quicker if I just do it myself".

If we're going to create a true business, with value and an exit strategy, we have to climb the ladder.

We'll discuss the tools needed to climb that ladder in Section 4. For now, it's worth noting the following. When we started our business, we had a set of skills, and a way of doing things. We could call that our recipe, and we'll talk much more about that later. To begin to ascend the entrepreneurial ladder, we need to realise that our clients are attracted to us because of that recipe. Thus, if we want to get more of the same sort of clients we have now, we need to make that recipe scalable. In other words, be able to recruit and train people to deliver our recipe in the same way as we do. Only then can we release ourselves from the comparatively low-value activities of doing the work of the business.

Manager

"I'm not very good at managing people". How many times do you think I have heard that?

Well, guess what? When you started (let's stick with the plumber idea), you probably weren't a great plumber either.

What made you great at what you do? Practice! So, why do you think that people believe that they aren't great managers? Because they don't practice enough! Instead of managing, they choose the Superman mindset, and that's a Mars bar choice if ever there was one.

The thing is, we don't manage people: we lead people, and manage systems. There's obviously a fundamental problem then when we consider management: in the large majority of businesses, there aren't many systems. We're going to talk much more about systems in Chapter 5, as they are the key to unlocking life and business freedom. For now, though, let's just agree that the definition of a system is a business process which is *written down*. If it's not written down, it's not a system.

Often, the "systems" that are there exist only in the head of the business owner (we called it the recipe earlier). They started the business with "their way of doing things" and it's got them to where they are now, employing a team – so it must work! The problem is, employees aren't very good at mind-reading, so it's very difficult for them to do things as well as the business owner if there's not a solid frame of reference for them to work to. Bear this in mind for now: the systems run the business, and the people run the systems. If we don't have systems (apart from in the owner's head) who's running the business?

Therefore, the first prerequisite for becoming a manager is to start to implement systems. Now, as we start to implement robust systems in our business, we start to create more scalability, as people can be trained to replicate our method of performing the tasks.

As a result, you start to create true leverage in your business, i.e. the ability to achieve more with less (specifically, less effort from you). While you still may have to perform some operational activities, you can now start to manage other people's activities to give you a predictable and consistent result. As a manager, therefore, you not only make money from your own activities, but also begin to make money from other people's activities. This is the start of your journey to freedom. Implementing robust systems will cause your belief that "no-one can do it as well as me" to shift to "my team can follow the system so that they *can* do it as well as me". It's a simple, yet seismic shift, which so many business owners I meet choose not to make. As a result, they're destined to that life of being tied to the lowest rung of their business.

However, should we choose to accept it's possible to create performances as good as ours in the operational aspects of our business, we can accelerate our journey towards that freedom that many covet. That's when we can ascend the E-ladder further and release ourselves from the time-for-money trap, once and for all. That's when we become a true business owner.

Business Owner

Here's where we start to have some more fun! How do business owners get paid? They receive dividends i.e. a distribution of profit from the business.

Think about this for a moment. It may be that you still have another role in your business, as well as being the business owner. But, essentially, if your money comes from dividends, we need to start thinking about your role in a different way.

Many people hold shares in FTSE companies, and expect to receive dividends in return for their investment. Makes sense, doesn't it? But how much time do they exchange working for the business in return for that dividend? That's right: precisely none!

There is absolutely no correlation between dividends and time. That means that you can receive a fantastic income, *and* not be tied to your business for 40, 50 or 60 hours per week. Without exception, *all* of the people we work with make more money and work less hours than before they started their coaching journey. In fact, some only visit their businesses a couple of times per week.

This, for many people, causes some confusion. In the same way that our social conditioning defines what "failure" means, it also defines our expectations with regards to exchange of time for something. Again, we were fed into the school system at five years old and expected to turn up at 8.30am every morning and leave at 4pm every evening. As we got older, the days got longer, and then we moved into employment where the days got longer still. We have been taught that work happens between 9am and 5pm, from Monday to Friday, and if we're not there during those hours, we're playing truant!

There's a pretty large paradox here, isn't there? As business owners, there should be no need to exchange time for money, as money comes from dividends. Though we may have some operational responsibilities, it's unlikely that we'd fill 40 hours a week if we were only performing high-value tasks (we're going to talk about time at some length next). But, because we have been conditioned to believe that a "good week's work" is 40 hours or more, it's not uncommon for me to meet a business owner who feels they have to find stuff to do in their business just to fill the time. Guilt has been mentioned to me on numerous occasions, i.e. people feeling guilty for working less than our socially accepted hours. This is where our ability to embrace the concept of freedom and doing less starts to fall over. We succumb to the vacuum (things expand to fill a vacuum, so we fill our week with low-value tasks). Unfortunately, this normally leads to some operational fires coming our way and, without discipline, this week becomes next week, and we find that we have only completed tasks that keep us where we are rather than those that *build* the business. Put yourself in the position of your team members. Do you think that they would prefer you to:

A) Be consistently present in the business doing lots of tasks which *they* could be doing for you (because that's why you employed them in the first place)?

Or,

B) Work a couple of days a week, or less, but on tasks that only you as the business owner can do, which means working *on* the business to move it forward, in turn ensuring that their jobs are safe?

I thought so!

I find it amazing how many clients tell me that they're not sure what makes up the role of the MD but then can give me a very clear description of the tasks that an MD performs. The truth is, they know *exactly* what an MD should be doing, but because it's not a job that takes much time (maybe as little as one day per week), it doesn't compute and they believe they are missing something.

The reality is, however, that running a business doesn't take very much time if it's organised properly. Until we accept that we don't have to trade 40 hours per week to sit in the MD's chair, we'll never fully embrace the idea of thinking smarter and achieving more with less.

Investor

When you have a business, you should now find yourself in a position where you are generating excess cashflow and have the time to do something with it. You can take that passive income and invest in property, shares or other businesses. As a business owner, you already know how to grow a commercial, profitable enterprise that works without you, so now you can replicate this as many times as you see fit. This affords you the opportunity to drastically accelerate your level of dreaming, as you are now receiving multiple streams of income with little exchange of time. At this point, you are still investing your own money, but are significantly leveraging its capability. There's one last step on the ladder though, and that's:

Entrepreneur

As a true entrepreneur, you create opportunities from other peoples' money. You are an idea generator and can leverage people and resources to create multiples of wealth. At this point, you aren't necessarily investing your money and time, but instead your level of knowledge and connections to create new opportunities. In reality, though, most people can create a life which affords them a fantastic level of life and business freedom before they reach this rung of the ladder.

Your focus right now should be to ascend to the level of business owner. Create one business which affords you the choices you want.

Just remember, once you have built one business, you can build any number.

SUMMARY

The principles I've discussed here are some of the key elements of smarter thinking; in other words, a high-performance mindset. Embrace them and use them. Teach them to others, and your level of understanding will deepen. On first read, they all seem pretty simple, don't they? As you practice the principles, however, you'll begin to notice just how deep they are, and how many nuances there are to each of them.

We've managed to build up a raft of strategies that guide your thinking and the language you use. Refer back to the first section, *The First Test*: we've put in place the thought processes to remove your interference and therefore increase the chance of elevating your performance and getting closer to that 10 that represents your potential.

We've established a set of tools to map out the life you want to achieve, work out how to get there and who you need to be to make it happen.

I guarantee that if you embrace the principles we've discussed, you *will* be more successful, and you *will* become the person to achieve your goals – even if they currently seem like they are a world away.

When we consider those interferences, the things that get in the way of us achieving our potential, we've left an elephant in the room; in fact, the number one excuse, the one used above all others. What do you think it is?

That's right: it's time. And that's why there's a whole section devoted to it.

Section 2: Doing Less: The Power of Time and Systems

"We must all suffer one of the two things: the pain of discipline or the pain of regret or disappointment."
Jim Rohn

Introduction

Time: our only finite resource. We should learn to use it better. When I speak at seminars, I spend a while talking about time and our relationship with it. I often ask the question, "How much *stupid* are you doing in your business right now?" Nods and smiles (and some groans of despair) usually reflect back at me from the assembled crowd. If we're really going to aim for life and business freedom then, once we've sorted out the way we think about our performance (using the principles from Section 1), we need to think about how we're acting. And that can only mean one thing: *not doing stupid!*

What's the key to using our time more efficiently? Systems! You see, we all already have systems in our lives to help us be more efficient and save time. I guarantee that, when you get in the shower every morning, you have a system. By that I mean a way of doing things in a prescribed order (which you probably aren't even conscious of anymore) which allows you to go from bath-mat to shower and back to bath-mat in the smoothest fashion possible.

In this section, we'll reframe your relationship with time so that you begin to treat it as your most valuable asset, and then arm you with the thinking to go and create efficiencies in your life and business like never before.

By the end, you'll have everything you need to start doing less.

Chapter 4

The Power of Time

INTRODUCTION

> *"The bad news is, time flies. The good news is, you're the pilot."*
> Michael Altshuler

Get obsessed with time!

We're going to talk about this at some length, as this is the biggest nut we have to crack if we're going to realise the power of smarter thinking and doing less.

It's also the number one excuse.

I can't even begin to count the number of times I've heard someone state that they haven't had time to get something done, or even that they don't have time to start a coaching programme because they're too busy.

In very simple terms, we all have the same number of hours available: we just need to choose to use them more wisely. But to use them wisely takes discipline, and a lot of it. It's so easy to allow in (what I call) "doing stupid", and by that, I mean wasting valuable time on activities with little or no value.

In this chapter, we'll reframe your relationship with time and get you to think about the impact of how you're choosing to use it right now. We'll discuss the highest impact strategies that will enable you to use your time better and start to achieve more with less.

However, it all stems from how you *think* about time, so we'd better start there.

Investing Time Versus Spending Time: Choose to Change or Choose to Stay the Same

In his book, *The 7 Habits of Highly Effective People*[1], Stephen Covey talks about time in the context of urgent and important, and maps this into a "Boston Box".

While useful, I prefer to think of it in this way:

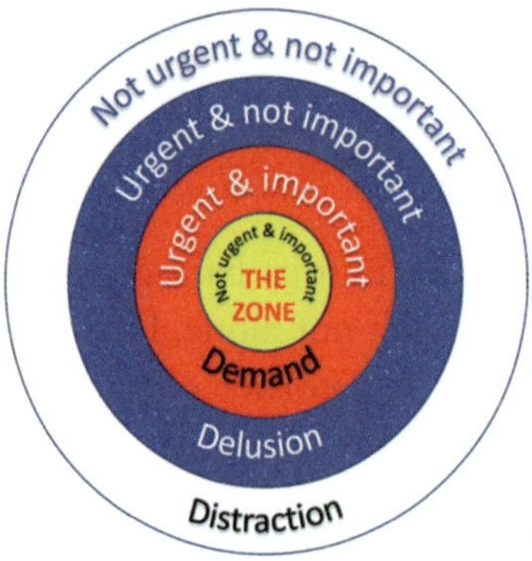

Figure 4.2: The time target

What does this remind you of? Yes, a target. And where do you normally want to hit a target?

The bullseye!

Of course, the bullseye is the smallest area on a target, which means it's the hardest to hit. It takes discipline and practice to consistently hit the bullseye. Without that practice, the chances of hitting one of the outer three rings instead is significantly increased.

The highest score happens when you hit the bullseye. And hitting the bullseye in your business is when you are doing activities to *build* the business, not doing the job of the business. As it says on

---

[1] *The 7 Habits of Highly Effective People*, Stephen R. Covey, Simon & Schuster UK; Reissue Edition (21 Nov. 2013)

the diagram, these may not feel urgent, but they are important! Let's now think about each of the segments.

Distraction

There are just so many distractions, aren't there? That's why it's the largest ring on the target and therefore the easiest to hit.

What's the biggest distraction in your day right now?

Does it look like this?

If you despair at the continuous barrage of emails hitting your inbox, then you're certainly not alone. How often do you let the little yellow envelope in the corner of your screen interrupt the task you're in the middle of?

Here's what often happens: the yellow envelope appears, and you stop what you're doing. You switch to your email application and read the email. You decide that you don't need to do anything with it *right* now. You then switch back to what you were originally doing and consider for a couple of minutes exactly where you were and how to get back into flow again. And there's the curse of email.

But, here's the thing: why do people send emails? There are, of course, a number of reasons, but let's really examine this for a moment. If you had something that needed doing *urgently*, would you send an email? I doubt it! Because, if you did, how would you know that the intended recipient was there to receive and act upon it? If it was urgent (and let's be fair, things rarely are), chances are that you'd pick up the phone instead. In my opinion, one of the big reasons that emails get sent is that it's a very easy way to clear out whatever is in your head at a point in time and offload it onto someone else so they can take care of it.

Another common distraction is the "got a minute?" meeting, where a team member arrives at your desk or office to unceremoniously butt into your day and ask a question.

The net effect of both of these is a disruption which knocks you off track and impacts your efficiency. Let's imagine that you receive 20 emails per day (it's probably more) and get interrupted for a "got a minute?" meeting 10 times per day. Apart from the physical time it takes to read the mail and realise that you don't need to do anything with it right now, and the time it takes to do the thinking for your employee who should be thinking for themselves, let's make a conservative estimate that, for each interruption, you take two minutes to get refocused. That's an hour gone each day, five hours per week, or around four weeks per year – just to get back into your flow after an interruption which you chose to allow in!

Imagine if you have been choosing to act that way for 10 years. One of those years (roughly) has been spent just trying to get refocused on what you should have been doing. Frightening, isn't it, when you start to really consider the impact?

Delusion

Let me give you a great example of delusion. It happened just after I started my business when, sitting at my desk one day, I decided that I *really needed* a binding machine. In my head, the binding machine would present my coaching programme agreements in a professional way, so it made complete sense. As a result of this thought, I proceeded to the Staples website, where I spent a good half an hour researching what I would need to create this favourable impression. Armed with my new knowledge, I jumped in the car and drove across town to the nearest Staples. Upon arrival, I was presented not only with the machines I'd seen on the website, but a couple of other options too. Half an hour of browsing later, I left Staples, the proud owner of a shiny new binding machine, and drove back across town to return to my desk. I then promptly placed the binding machine in the cupboard, since I didn't actually have any prospects in the pipeline to go and present my professionally bound programme agreements to!

And that, my friends, is a fantastic example of delusion. The thing which appears to be the most urgent often carries absolutely no importance whatsoever. Why is it then that we are so good at discovering such opportunities?

What delusions are you finding in your day? And what's the reason for it? Is it so you don't have to go and address the stuff that really needs addressing, because that might be right at the edge of, or outside of, your comfort zone? Sounds like we may be heading off in that below the line of choice direction now, doesn't it?

Demand

Of course, demand is the thing which tends to eat most of our time most consistently (if we choose to allow it). The day-to-day operational firefighting which causes us to get to the end of our day and state, "I was really busy today", but not really be able to list out what we did. The challenge here is that there will always be more operational fires to put out, team challenges to solve, and customer queries to answer. If there aren't those things going on in your business, then I'd be pretty worried. But the point is, that's not your job! Unless we are really disciplined with the choices we make around time, we'll never get in the Zone.

There's a really important point here. When we're working *in* our business, we're only really doing tasks to stand still and stay the same. We have to be working *on* our business in order to create change.

The Zone

The Zone is where we move towards our goals. We're choosing to work *on* our business, instead of *in* it. To be able to do that successfully, we need to have the elements in place that we discussed in Section 2, i.e. clear goals and a clear plan. Otherwise, we can put time aside to work on our business, but not know what to do or how to prioritise our tasks in that time to really gain traction. Consequently, our *on* time tends to get put aside for *in* time because we know exactly what needs doing there, and it's shouting louder.

At this point, it would seem fitting to wander off on a bit of a tangent as, if we're really going to get a handle on our time, then don't we need to be thinking about it differently?

You Are Your Most Important Customer

Who is the most important customer in your business right now?

When I ask this question to most people, they reel off a list of their biggest, favourite or most profitable customers.

Yes, they're important. But they're not the *most* important. The way most people behave, however, would tend to indicate that they see their customer as the most important person in their life. Why? Because when the customer calls and asks to see them the next day, they immediately drop everything and go.

Who then, I hear you ask, *is* the most important?

Let me explain. Think about the structure of your business. Whether you have people in these roles, or you're wearing multiple hats, you'll probably have an organisational structure that looks something like this:

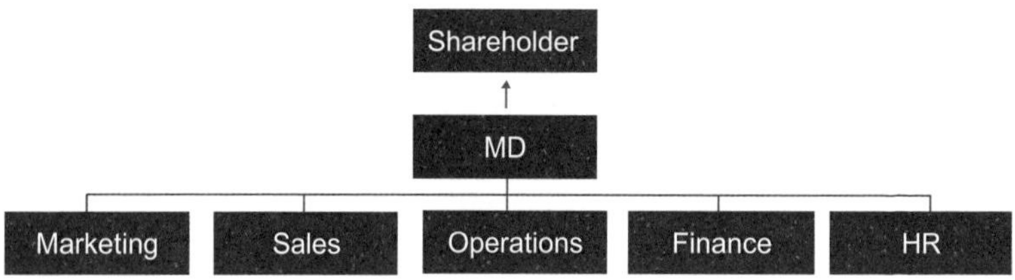

Figure 4.3: Organisational chart

You're the MD of the business, (even if you're not currently choosing to sit in that seat very often). This means that you're responsible for ensuring that the business runs smoothly, as close to plan as possible, and that each of your department heads are doing what they should be doing (even if some of them are you).

That's the operating element of the business. But, as the MD, you're also responsible for serving your shareholder. And your shareholder is looking for you, as the MD, to be delivering value and return on investment. While you're sitting in the MD chair, you're serving your shareholder, and they are the most important customer in your business right now as they are the only person you can't replace. This then makes them, most definitely, your most important customer.

If you plan to deliver better value to your shareholder, therefore, it surely makes sense that a proportion of your time is consistently applied to creating value in your business. Not the one-off value of a customer transaction, because that simply keeps the wheels of your business turning and heading in the same direction. Instead I mean the exponential value that you create by improving the way that your business runs, the working *on* rather than *in* element. That is the time that creates value in your business, giving you more consistency and predictability, and ultimately more freedom and the choice to do less and achieve more.

With that in mind, what proportion of your week are you currently investing in serving your most important customer?

More importantly, let's think about this: if you were in a meeting with a customer, would you allow yourself to be distracted by emails, phone calls or team members arriving unannounced to interrupt you?

Of course not!

Now that we've established that *you* are your most important customer, consider how often you've allowed distractions into the time when you're moving your business forward? I'm guessing that, for most people, the answer is "most of the time".

Here's the most important point: when the email arrives, or your customer calls to request that you drop everything and go and see them, who is the only person who knows what's going on in your diary?

YOU!

Would the sender of the email, or your customer, expect you to answer their call or email if you were already in a meeting with a customer? Probably not. How do they know what your diary looks like when they call up to request that you drop everything and go and see them? Would it be fair to say that most reasonable people, if presented with, "I can't make tomorrow as I already have a meeting scheduled", would respond with something along the lines of, "That's OK, when can you make it?", or something similar?

What is the lesson here? You're in control of your time. It's sloppy choices that lead us to be inefficient, nothing more. You're the only person who can choose whether to look at the email the moment it arrives or drop everything to go and see your customer. You cannot blame the sender. If you don't like the choices that you're making around time right now, change them.

If your most important customer is your shareholder, put yourself in their shoes now, and consider this question:

Is the person responsible for creating the value I'm looking for in my business doing a great job, and would I rehire them?

If not, it's time to start getting much more disciplined with your time. We'll discuss the top tips for this later, but first I'd just like to ram this point home for you.

A Reality Check: The COAGulator

I love using this tool with clients as it normally jolts them quite drastically into thinking differently about their time. It's a calculator which estimates your chances of staying the same or getting stuck.

Here's the meaning of coagulate: "Change to a solid or semi-solid state". In other words, when something coagulates, nothing moves anymore.

1. I'd like you to do a rough estimation of your week, and complete the following table (I've put in some example numbers):

Working weeks per year	A	50
Hours per week	B	40
Years until exit/major goal	C	5
HOURS TOTAL (A x B x C)	D	10,000

Figure 4.4: Calculation of total hours to goal

Great, so we now have the total number of hours (D) available to us to achieve either an exit from our business or a major goal.

2. Next, complete the following table, carefully thinking about how you allocate your time currently.You'll need to refer to the time target for this one (figure 4.2). Blame, excuses or denial are categorically not allowed when completing this part.

Time sector	Examples	% of week
Distraction	Email, "got a minute?" meetings, phone calls	
Delusion	Football scores Facebook, (Staples visits!)	
Demand	Working *in* your business i.e. operational firefighting, day-to-day tasks	
The Zone	Working *in* your business i.e. planning, strategy, managing functional heads	
	TOTAL (E)	100%

Figure 4.5: Time apportionment

We've agreed that the only area of the time target which will cause a change to happen is the Zone, as all three other areas are there just to get us through the day and keep us where we are; in other words, in a solid or semi-solid state.

The last stage is therefore to take the number from the hours total box (D) from figure 4.4 and multiply it by the percentage you allocated in the Zone box (E) from figure 4.5. Let's say you allocated 5% of your time in the Zone, and we apply it to my time example above:

10,000 hours x 5% = 500 hours

Congratulations!

You now have your COAGulator score, i.e. the number of hours you'll allocate to your business exit or major goal over that time period if you continue to behave as you currently are!

How would you rate your chances of success right now?

And that's why we call it the COAGulator: because it's a *calculator* to estimate your Chance Of Achieving your Goals!

The lower your percentage of time in the Zone and the lower the chance you've got. In other words, the higher your likelihood of getting stuck!

I've not met too many people who have completed that exercise, and still backed themselves to hit their goals. How did you fair?

But don't get despondent. Now you are aware of how you are choosing to use your time, and other choices are still available.

Let's go back to the idea of choosing your activities and relate it to the hours you just worked out. You'll have a number of hours you predicted that you'd work each year.

At this point, I'd like you to take your goal income, let's say £100,000 for example, and divide it by the number of hours you're saying you'll work.

Let's use the figures from the previous example: 40 hours per week for 50 weeks per year. If you divide goal income by hours, you'll have an hourly rate. (I understand that we said earlier that income didn't correlate with time, but this is purely to act as a placeholder in your mind).

Here, the hourly rate is £50. (£100,000 divided by 2,000 hours). What's your desired hourly rate? More importantly, what proportion of your week are you actually spending working at that rate? If it's like many of the people I start to work with, the answer will be a low number.

But, here's the *really* interesting thing. Take the number of hours you're working, and then break them down into an estimated hourly rate for the tasks you're doing, like this:

Hours per week (A)	Weeks per year (B)	Total hours AxB= (C)	Task	Hourly rate of task (D)	Value CxD (E)
8	50	400	Admin	£8	£3,200
24	50	1,200	Operational work	£10	£12,000
4	50	200	Mopping up after team	£10	£2,000
4	50	200	Managing the business		£10,000
40		2,000	TOTAL		£27,200

You'll come up with a number at the bottom of column E which equates to a time-apportioned value of how you're choosing to use your time. How different does that look from what you're actually paying yourself?

When I've run this exercise with clients, it's frightening just how close the number is to what they are actually paying themselves.

Here's the point: if you're choosing to undertake tasks at a low hourly rate, how do you ever expect to make a high hourly rate?

We need to examine this more closely.

The Fun/Skill Matrix: Focusing on High Value Tasks or "Doing Stupid"?

Now I've used the COAGulator to get your attention, let's look at a practical tool where you can keep an easy piece of language in your head to continuously evaluate how you're choosing to spend your time.

It's called the fun/skill matrix. (figure 4.6) You'll see it's a 3x3 grid made up of two components: level of interest, and level of skill the task requires and therefore the potential value it adds to the organisation. In the top right corner, you'll see the "orange" box represented by diagonal lines. It's the highest value box in the matrix. In the bottom left hand corner is the "green" box, represented by horizontal lines.

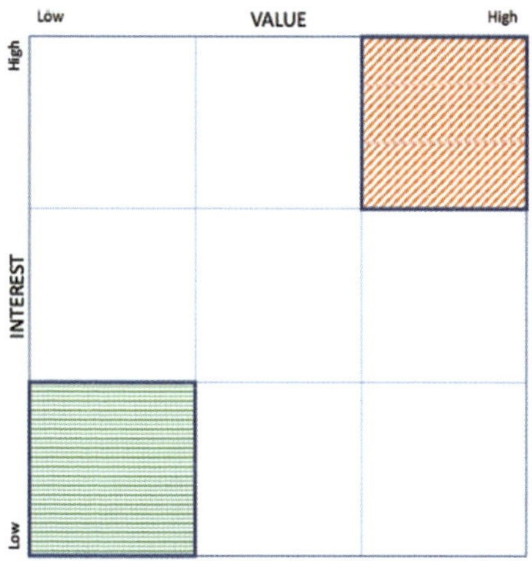

Figure 4.6: The fun/skill matrix

Everyone in your organisation has an orange box and a green box. The orange box is made up of all the tasks you hired them to perform. It would be the list of tasks that would answer the question, "What does a great day look like for this person?"

Conversely, the green box represents all the low-value tasks which sit in delusion or distraction, and sometimes even in the demand area.

How we choose to allocate our time is the key. Let's look at an example. One of the clients I worked with had a production manager, earning around £35,000 per year. If we take the hourly rate on that, it's around £17 per hour. The guys on the shop floor were earning £8-£9 per hour.

This particular manager loved being on the shop floor, making the parts for customers and generally rolling up his sleeves and getting stuck in. Now, while on the one hand you could argue that this was a great attitude as he really wanted to help his team get the work done, we need to consider it from a different perspective.

As the manager, his high-value tasks were such things as scheduling the workflow, proactively communicating with customers to ensure that their expectations were met, analysing the profitability of jobs to ensure that they were being costed correctly and organising preventative maintenance for the machinery to minimise downtime. These tasks represented his orange box, the things that he was employed to do, and the things that only he (apart from the owner of the business) had the skills to do.

But, because they were really busy, he *had* (in his mind) to work on the shop floor to get the work out on time.

The point is this: they were *always* really busy, so he was *always* on the shop floor. As a result, he said he just "didn't have the time" to do all the important stuff which he was employed to do! And there came the excuse (back to below the line thinking from Section 1.)

He was choosing green box activities, the really low-value tasks (for him) instead of choosing the tasks he should have been doing. Why? Because they were easy! They were in his comfort zone, and he didn't have to think about them too hard. But it meant that we had a really high paid member of the team doing comparatively low-value work.

The challenge was the impact this had throughout the whole business. The owner had to step back to mop up after him and do the tasks he should have been doing. Of course, these tasks didn't represent a great use of time for the owner, as it prevented him from doing what only *he* could do, such as going out and seeing customers and new prospects to generate sales. That suited *him* fine because that was *his* comfort zone, so it became easy to collude with the production manager to avoid his own orange box tasks.

I've seen numerous examples of this in my time working with clients. The challenge is that, in these instances, the whole situation plays to the idea of the Superman syndrome we talked about earlier: the owner feels like he can step in and save the day.

But, the harsh reality is, when this happens in an organisation, the negative effects are felt throughout. When team members are working below their hourly rate, the *really* important tasks aren't being done and, as a result, the whole business is both inefficient and ineffective.

We'll talk more about the toolkit we can use to define everyone's orange boxes later. For the time being, embed it as a piece of language for yourself. It's a really easy question for you to ask yourself on a regular basis: "Is this task in my orange box?" If the answer is "No", stop doing it as soon as possible, because that's called doing stupid!

How a Scarcity Mentality Prevents Business Freedom: "Saving a Wage is Costing You a Fortune"

In 2007, I went to a seminar that Brad Sugars, founder of ActionCOACH, was giving, and this was one of the quotes that stuck in my head:

"Saving a wage is costing you a fortune".

If you consider the example above, we established that the production manager "had to" work on the shop floor because they were always so busy. We also established that the guys on the shop floor were earning £8 or £9 per hour. If we look at this completely logically, therefore, for just over £300 per week, we could hire another team member for the shop floor, and the production manager's time is now freed up to perform his orange box tasks as we listed earlier. Effectively, he would now be working at his hourly rate of £17, doing the tasks that he was both employed to do and skilled in doing. Not only that, the business owner will free up a significant proportion of *his* time to do the tasks that, at the time, only *he* could do, such as go out and find new customers to grow the business.

But none of that was happening because they "simply couldn't afford another £18,000 of wages"!

And this is the problem. When we're thinking about a salary, we always think of the *big* number, i.e. £18,000 per year, and not the small number of £9 per hour. As a result, fear (False Expectations Appearing Real) kicks in, we hit the point of discomfort, and decide that we already have enough resource to get the job done, so we won't hire anyone right now! Hence, it perpetuates, with everyone in the business working inefficiently below their hourly rate for most of the time.

And that, my business owner friend, is the trap that will tie you the metaphorical shop floor of your business, as you're spending all your time mopping up after people who aren't doing their job. I'm afraid that, with these choices, you can never experience freedom from your business; you'll always be looking over your shoulder, waiting for the next ball to drop, doing more and not less.

Sadly, this is the reason that many business owners have given me as to why they once had a team, but they've gone back to doing it themselves because it's easier, they can do it better, and more quickly.

Here's another of Brad's quotes from the seminar I mentioned earlier:

> *"Poor people spend time to save money. Wealthy people spend money to save time".*

At the time, I thought to myself: "That's all very well for you; you're already wealthy, so you can afford to say that". But wealthy isn't a status, it's a mindset. How can you ever *become* wealthy if you choose to act in the way described above?

If you're choosing to consume your time with low-value tasks because, in your perception, you can't afford to hire someone to do them, you're tying yourself to the treadmill of your business, ever destined to trade too many hours for not enough money and drive yourself towards burnout. When you're thinking that you can't afford to hire someone, the reality is *you can't afford not to*!

How many sales would you need to generate to cover a person's wage for a day or week? We'll get into this in more detail later, when we look at the numbers in your business. The key point is that, if you hire someone, it normally allows you not only to free up your time to work on the business to bring more work through the door and make it run more efficiently, but also to still have time left over to do the other things you want to do. Here's where we plant the seeds of freedom.

Schedule Your Priorities, Don't Prioritise Your Schedule

We looked at the time target earlier (figure 4.2). Let's look at it again from a different perspective. Instead of a target, imagine that you're looking down into a hole! Perspective means that the centre circle (the Zone) is the deepest point in the hole. Now imagine that the other circles in the hole represent points in the hole closer and closer to the surface (it's much easier after all to sit at the edge of a hole and dangle your legs into it (distraction) than climb to the bottom (the Zone). Unfortunately, the walls of the hole are walls of sand. They're always spilling over into the hole and covering the bottom (the Zone) until it's not visible anymore and has become consumed by distraction, delusion and demand.

In short, therefore, the activities that you identify as orange activities need fierce protection. The green box tasks will just keep coming and coming; there'll be more of them than we can ever get done and there will never be an endpoint. As a result, the orange box tasks take a back seat, time goes by, and we don't move forward.

What would you do to stop walls of sand encroaching on an area? Build a wall around it, of course!

How then, do we build a wall around our time? We call it a default diary (and we'll do an exercise to create one soon). Create blocks of time in your diary when specific activities *have* to take place, and then *do* them. This means you have to *be* disciplined. Only you can choose whether to be disciplined or not.

The main concept here is this: schedule your priorities, don't prioritise your schedule.

In other words, there's not much point taking your task list and ranking it in order of importance if you're not including the truly important tasks which are required to move your business forward.

It's easy to ring-fence some time in your diary and mark it up as "working on my business" but, unless you're really clear of the activity you're going to perform in that slot, it's unlikely to be a fruitful use of time. You'll arrive at your designated slot of time, look at your diary, spend a couple of minutes wondering how you'll fill the time, and then go and do the more pressing operational (demand-based) activities which are shouting louder because they really need doing. You won't know where to start.

I'll therefore refer you back to the earlier section, specifically the success formula in Chapter 3. There is a very strong correlation between planning and the efficient use of a block of time to work *on* your business.

Of course, to help create space for orange boxes, we need to identify the green stuff which might be getting in the way. Earlier, I mentioned emails and the "got a minute?" meetings. Let's deal with these in turn.

Creating the Space to Schedule Your Priorities

If your day looks like that of many of the people I coach, you'll have distraction, delusion and demand coming at you from every angle. If we're going to create the space to schedule your priorities, the high-value tasks, then we need to minimise the impact of the low-value tasks. We can do this by batching them up and doing them all together as it will keep the task focused and efficient. In other words, these need to become a part of your default diary too.

Let's take two of the biggest distractions that we've already talked about: emails and "got a minute?" interruptions from your team. How can you minimise their impact on your day?

Emails

As we've already discussed, emails can be a huge distraction in our day. To an extent, phone calls fall into the same category. We could, however, choose to do them in a more efficient manner. Both email and telephone calls need to be dealt with, there's no doubt about that. But, as our inbox forms a receptacle for emails, we also have a receptacle for phone calls; it's called voicemail. These receptacles store them for you precisely so that you *don't* have to deal with them as soon as they arrive.

Block out a chunk of time where you will allow yourself to check email and voicemails. This may be once a day, perhaps twice or maybe even three times. You'll know the right frequency depending on your business (you may need more voicemail sessions than email sessions). On some email systems, you can choose when the server delivers the email, so it is possible to remove the opportunity for distraction entirely. Remember that only you know what you are doing at any point in the day. In reality, your client or customer shouldn't be expecting an immediate response to email as they are, in general, a low priority form of communication.

"Got a Minute?" Meetings

When your team member turns up at your door and opens with the question, "Got a minute?", what's that really saying? For the most part, this is what my clients have found: it means that the team member has a problem which they're not sure about. Rather than think about it themselves, they'd prefer to pass it on to you so that a) they don't have to think about it anymore, and, b) if it goes wrong and it was your idea, it wasn't their fault.

The question is that, in 80% of cases, could the team member have solved the problem for themselves? I've found the answer is categorically "yes". But, instead of teaching them to think about it, many of us choose to don the Superman cape and solve it ourselves, hence teaching the team member that, whenever they encounter a challenge which is going to take more than the usual amount of thought, they should bring it to us so we can sort it out for them.

Without exception, the following strategy has worked with all of the business owners I work with. Block out a section of time in your day (let's say half an hour after lunch from 1.30pm until 2pm, for example). Tell your team members that this is the period of time when you are available to answer their queries. Ask them to save them up until then so you can help them sort them out all at once.

Most importantly, stick to this. If they arrive outside of the allotted time, send them away again until the next session.

When they do arrive at the allotted time, rather than *tell* them what to do, *ask* them what *they* think they should do. Get them to give you a couple of options, then ask them to decide. As long as the decision moves them forward, let them do it. At all costs, resist the temptation to solve the problem for them, as this only teaches them that you are still the answer to their challenges and ready to don that old Superman cape again! Only in exceptional cases should you step in to add some further knowledge to the situation so that they can make a better decision. Otherwise, just ask more questions so that they continue to think for themselves. I know now that you're thinking, "I don't have time for that. It's far quicker and easier to tell them". But stick with it, because what we are really doing here is re-educating people to think for themselves and have more confidence in their own decision-making.

Guess what happens next? 80% of your interruptions disappear. Why? Because your team are actually capable of solving the problem themselves. The 20% of challenges that still get presented to you are the key ones where the team member will still need further education to create the best outcome. When you ask them questions and then ratify their decision, confidence grows and, over time, they will not only bring you their challenge, but also a couple of robust solutions and their suggestion for which to pursue.

I've worked this system for years with clients. Here's the way it plays out. They start with numerous "got a minute?" interruptions.

They block out half an hour in their diary every day and strictly reinforce the need to stick to that time slot only. The number of queries vastly reduces, almost overnight.

After a couple of weeks, the need for a daily block of time miraculously disappears. In fact, most end up only having a weekly block of time, and the team just get on with it. How much time would that save you every week if you chose to do the same?

Let's just take those two ideas and imagine you stick to them with fastidious discipline. How much time would you save every week, as a result? I've had clients who have saved a day or more! And it's a day that was just being filled up with distraction and delusion. What could you be doing with that time to redress the balance on your COAGulator?

Create a Default Diary

Take a piece of paper and make a list of all the activities that you perform on a daily, weekly and monthly basis. Now, put a rough hourly rate next to them: that is the amount you'd have to pay someone to complete the task.

It should start to become apparent which are your orange box activities. These include essential daily, weekly and monthly tasks which only you can do (managing your direct reports, analysing the numbers in your business, planning for the future, etc.). Include the tasks which you know you *should* be doing, i.e. the ones which are really important to the development of the business, but which aren't currently being done either at all or on a consistent basis because "there's never time".

Take a green highlighter pen, and strike through the items which are the lowest value (let's say these are the ones for which you could pay someone £10 per hour). Your first job is either to delegate them or hire someone to do them.

Remember the idea that we discussed earlier: how many sales do you need to make to cover the wage of a £10 per hour person? Let's say you have a margin of 25%, and someone works 7.5 hours per day. To cover their £75, you need to generate a margin equivalent to that, which represents a sale of £300, at this margin. How many sales, on average, does that represent for you? Consider how long you perceive it will take you to generate that level of sales compared to the amount of time it's saved you by hiring that person, and you've now truly experienced the idea of "saving a wage is costing you a fortune".

Next, take an orange pen, and highlight all the tasks which are the highest value and that you perceive that only you can or should be doing. (It's time to get above the line here and remember that your Superman cape needs to stay firmly in the cupboard).

Once you've crystallised the orange activities, take your diary, preferably an electronic calendar, and set up a recurring block of time for each of these tasks. Right now, you may over or underestimate the time you require as, for the most part, you may not have been doing these activities in a focused and disciplined way. That's OK, you can fine tune later. The important thing is that you have the placeholder in your diary for the activity. Next, create the recurring blocks of time to deal with the batched, low-value activities we talked about (email and interruptions).

Congratulations!

You have now successfully scheduled your priorities and made the low-value activities efficient. It's now your job to stick to that diary. No excuses! (By the way, you are allowed to move an orange box entry, but not delete it).

Teach your team that, during these default diary times, you are unavailable (unless it's management time with them of course), and voraciously protect your orange box!

You'll notice that there are probably some tasks on your list that you haven't coloured orange or green. They're the tasks which you'd have to pay someone a bit more to do, but which probably don't make up part of your optimum role. You have a number of choices with these activities. Obviously, the eventual outcome needs to be that you pass them on to someone else. It may be that you'll need to hire that person, but they're not in your budget yet. It may be that you can pass it on, but it needs a system to be wrapped around it first, and someone in the business needs to be trained to get the task done effectively. Both of those options are OK. Just plan how you're going to do it and over what period of time. Then schedule a non-recurring orange box activity in your diary.

For the time being, should you need to continue to do these tasks, it's your job to get them done as efficiently and effectively as possible. So, once again, batch them in default diary blocks so that you stay focused and the task doesn't sprawl into your diary like a spider stretching out its legs!

I can promise you that, without exception, everyone who has had the discipline to do this task and follow through on it consistently, has saved multiple hours per week, become more efficient, grown their business faster *and* had more personal time.

Sounds like a plan, doesn't it?

Practical Tips to Maximise Your Time

We've established that time is a question of discipline.

This really is the most important thing to embed when we start to think about using our time more effectively. We've talked about email disruption and the "got a minute?" meetings, where team members will arrive unannounced at your door to unload their challenges on to you. We've also agreed this: only *you* know what is happening in your diary at any point in time, so it's up to *you* as to whether you allow the distraction of email, phone calls, team members or even customers requesting that you jump in the car at their beck and call to go and see them.

By now, hopefully, you've made the choice to get more protective of your time and stop "doing stupid".

We should be in a place where the orange box activities are protected by a placeholder in your diary, the green box activities are gone, and those in between are batched (and part of a plan) to be delegated at some point in the near future.

How can we build on our effectiveness, then? Here are a couple of top tips to maximise your time.

There's a fantastic book called *Eat That Frog*[2] by Brian Tracy. The frog is the horrible but most important thing that needs doing every day (it may be calling a customer, for example, to collect an overdue invoice). Make it the first thing you do, i.e. "Eat the frog for breakfast"! This will stop you procrastinating for the rest of the day, looking for excuses not to do that task.

Make a to-do list of activities for the next day, every evening, before you finish (you could have a default diary entry set up on a daily recurring basis, entitled "plan tomorrow"). Once you have made the list, prioritise it in terms of importance. These are the key activities which need to happen around your already scheduled orange box activities. The benefits of this are that, when you arrive the next day, you don't waste any time thinking about what it is you need to do, with your tasks already prioritised. There's also another benefit. When you write something down, your subconscious can relax, as it knows you've captured the task. Not only that, it works on the task subconsciously for you. How often have you gone to bed with a problem and woken up with the solution? Solving problems while you sleep seems like a fantastic time-saving plan to me!

SUMMARY

When you're working in your orange box, you're moving forward. When you're not, you're staying rooted in the same spot.

If you've got to this point in the book, and you've not done the exercise to create a default diary, stop now and do it before you read any further. Remember, if you're not disciplined with your time, why would you expect your team to be? They all have orange boxes too, and the reason you've employed them, at the rate you're paying them, is to be in that orange box for the largest proportion of time possible.

We should now be in a place where we're thinking in a high-performance way, with clear goals for ourselves and the business.

---

[2] *Eat That Frog! 21 Great Ways to Stop Procrastinating and Get More Done in Less Time*, Brian Tracy, Mc-Graw Hill Education, 2017

We should have a plan in place, even if that's only a list of tasks which need to be undertaken by a specific date. As a result, we should be getting better at acting in a way which will move the business forward.

Remember that all the principles we've talked about with regard to mindset and time also apply to team if you really want an organisation which operates efficiently, effectively and gives you the opportunity to experience life and business freedom.

Now it's time to focus on the vehicle which brings you true leverage in your business.

Let's move then on to systems.

Chapter 5

The Power of Systems: Your Route to Freedom

> *"Teamwork is the ability to work together toward a common vision. The ability to direct individual accomplishments toward organizational objectives. It is the fuel that allows common people to attain uncommon results".*
>
> – Andrew Carnegie

INTRODUCTION

It's a very simple fact: you can't have a world-class business without a world-class team. And you certainly won't achieve the life and business freedom you want without a team who are truly on board with you and where you are going. But, to have a world-class team, you'll also need great systems. After all, they're the thing that allows your business to run smoothly, consistently and become scalable.

It's one of your primary roles as the owner of the business; to ensure that you have the right team on your bus, in the right seats, playing to their strengths and operating at their highest level of value (in the orange box) for as much of their time as possible.

I often ask this question of clients I work with:

"What does a great day look like for this person in your business?" Then I follow with:

"If I asked them the same question, would they give me the same answer?"

I'm sure you can probably guess what the answer comes back as.

The reality is that, in most businesses, the team really aren't that clear on what their great day should look like. They have no real accountability, no systems to operate and no clear feedback and management loop to help them improve. Unfortunately, this can often result in the business owner starting to take a negative view of the team member (through no real fault of the employee).

It can also lead to Superman syndrome (as discussed earlier) kicking in for the owner: "Well, they aren't capable of doing the job, so it's easier if I just get on and do it".

I call this "wriggle room". In the absence of clarity around the direction of the business, the team members' role in that, what their measurable deliverables are, and systems and processes to provide for consistent delivery of the product or service, all manner of chaos can ensue.

In essence, then, the idea must be to *take away* the wriggle room. In order to do that, we must remove the subjectivity from the business, and make it as objective as possible. We therefore deploy systems. As we've mentioned before: the systems run the business and the people run the systems.

Systems are all about creating leverage in your business. It's a concept that few truly understand, so let's look in detail at it now.

The Secret of Less is More: Leverage

> *"Leverage is the reason some people become rich and others do not."*
> Robert Kiyosaki

If you're truly ready to embrace the idea of life and business freedom, then there's really only one word we need to fixate on:

LEVERAGE.

What is leverage?
The key to business success!
What does it mean?

In essence, there are three meanings. We'll talk about each in more detail as we go through this section, but let's get the three definitions clear first.

1. Divide to multiply. For example, when we hire a team, we divide the tasks among them to allow specialisation, and so people can play to their strengths more of the time.

2. Less is more. If you've come across the 80:20 rule, then less is *always* more. For example, 20% of your customers will account for roughly 80% of your profit. Similarly, 20% of your customers account for 80% of your headaches! (Why not let them be someone else's customer instead?)

   And, most likely, 20% of the tasks you do will create 80% of the value in your business (orange box).

That's two definitions of leverage. Here's the most important and valuable one though:

3. Do the work once and get paid forever.

Think about this for a moment. Many of the people I work with have used the excuse that it's just easier, faster, better if they do it because blah, blah (insert excuses). That's a great example of doing the work once and getting paid once; and that's just dumb.

We've talked about this trap in the section on the entrepreneurial ladder. Doing the "shop floor" work in your business simply isn't your job. Because, if you're doing *that* job, who is doing the MD's job?

What, then, does "doing the work once and getting paid forever" really mean? In the context of business, it means putting the systems in place to create consistent, reliable and predictable outputs.

As I've said previously, we *manage* systems and *lead* people. For our business to work consistently well, we need to be able to delegate (and not abdicate) tasks to our team. But there's an obvious prerequisite for *delegation*, and that is systems and processes. If we systematise the business once, we can use the systems…forever. Sure, they will need some modification from time to time, but who are the best people to do that? The team, of course. And that's another example of leverage.

The faster we learn to think in terms of leverage in our business, the faster we progress. In the last section of the book, therefore, I'm going to concentrate on the concepts which will give you the most leverage, because that feeds the "less is more" mindset, doesn't it?

Systems in Your Business: What Are They and Why Are They Important?

When we're considering someone's ability to perform their role well, our first stop should be to look to the system. Is there a system, or are we just expecting someone to turn up and do what they think they should? Next, how well have they been trained in the system? Of course, if no system exists then we know the answer to that! The *last* place to look is to the actual employee. If we don't give them an agreed way of doing things and train them in it, how can we possibly expect them to perform?

We'll discuss this at length later but, as a prelude to that, remember what system stands for:

S ave
Y ourself
S tress
T ime
E nergy, and
M oney

The rules are that, until it's written, it's not a system. I say written because, if it's not written, it's open to interpretation, which can lead to inconsistency. For us to have a solid base to build on, we are looking for consistency.

We could also call systems a performance standard. If the criteria of the system are met, then performance is as expected. When those criteria are not met, performance is below standard.

As the business owner, you are the guardian of the systems in your business. It's your responsibility to ensure that the business operates to a clearly documented system for a number of reasons.

First, in the absence of a system, you can't possibly blame the team for their results, as you didn't supply an agreed way of doing things. Thus, they'll all be doing their jobs their own way, with best intentions, but that may not get you the results you want.

Second, the value of your business lies in your systems. Remember that the systems run the business and every new employee should be trained to become competent in *your* business. That's what creates a scalable, consistent enterprise. You can sell your business system; look at how much you invest in a McDonald's franchise which comes with no team members. What it does come with is a world-class operating system which enables the new franchisee to rapidly start a new business and achieve McDonald's required standards with a team of inexperienced 16 and 17-year-olds.

By introducing systems into your business, a common level of understanding is achieved. There is a homogenised "way things are done around here". This makes your business *objective*. By that I mean, since we are referencing an agreed performance standard, the element of emotion is removed and, therefore, when people are held accountable to the systems, it's not personal. We are looking to catch the behaviour that doesn't meet the required performance standards and improve it; and recognise the behaviour that exceeds those standards and reinforce it.

Until the systems are documented, inconsistency is usually rife in a business, and decisions become more *subjective*, i.e. open to personal interpretation. As a result, people take things more personally, are more defensive (usually) and therefore have more propensity to dip into below that line thinking.

The Nine Ways to Systematise Your Business: The Route to Business Freedom and a High-performing Team

There are nine key factors in systematising a business, and they are key to getting a team performing at a high level.

Let's get an idea of the nine elements, and then examine them individually:

1. Vision
2. Mission
3. Culture
4. Goals
5. Organisational chart
6. Positional contracts
7. Key performance indicators
8. How-to manuals
9. Management systems

When I talk about them with my clients, I often use a sporting analogy. Let's take the English rugby team as an example. (It doesn't matter if you're not a rugby fan, by the way, as this metaphor can apply to any sport). Let's have a look at this example now, and then we'll dig into each a bit deeper.

Vision

Vision is the guiding light for your business. It sets the direction of where you are heading, and it should inspire and engage your team. For the England team, their vision could be: "To be the best rugby team in the world". If your team aren't excited by your vision, why are they on your bus? If you don't have a vision, what have they got to be inspired by?

Mission

Your mission is the roadmap to your vision, i.e. how you will accomplish your vision. There are four key elements within your mission:

1. Who you are.
2. What business you are in.
3. Who your customers are.
4. What makes you different.

For the England team, the mission could be something like:

> "We are the world's number one rugby team, committed to the pursuit of excellence in every aspect of the sport, both on and off the field. We inspire young people to play sport and aim for the highest level of achievement. Our fans are passionate about the game of rugby and all our efforts are directed at providing them with excitement, satisfaction and pride in their team."

The mission starts to create more alignment around the vision by building more specificity into it.

Culture

A culture statement is a set of values which are evidenced by behaviour. At the heart of the business should be a set of core values, i.e. the marketplace, when describing your business, would say: "They're the guys who…"

The England team's culture could include elements such as excellence, commitment and communication. This culture would be brought to life through stories, to embed the meaning of those values.

Goals

We've discussed goals already, at some length, and they are obviously key strategic milestones which are aligned with your vision.

For the England team, the goals could be: "Win the Six Nations", or, "Win the World Cup".

In my opinion, the four areas outlined above are the leadership elements of the nine key factors in systematising your business. These four elements create the environment and align the team to ensure that everyone is on the same page, heading in the same direction and operating with the same values. The goals then start to create the bridge to the management of the business.

If we consider the England team, we now have a bunch of well-aligned individuals with a common goal, standing on a pitch but not knowing what to do.

Therefore, we not only need a leadership aspect, but also a management focus, and here's where the other five key points come in.

Organisational chart

If we've got an aligned team then, of course, we need a team sheet. There are lots of different positions on the field which make up a game of rugby, and there are reporting lines: the team reports to the captain, and there's normally someone in charge of the forwards. Can you imagine all 15 members of the team running around the pitch without a clear definition of what their position is? It's the same in the game of business: there are definite positions and functions which need to be addressed in order to fulfil all the aspects of the game. We need to define them on an organisational chart to make sure they are clear.

Positional contracts

Of course, it's fine to have a team sheet, or organisational chart, but it's not much use unless the roles are defined. There are 15 positions on a rugby team, and each has a different role in the game. It's the hooker's job, for example, to win the ball in the scrum, and feed it into the lineout. They also need to be involved in the breakdowns. Conversely, the full-back is all about defence and his main role is to get the ball when kicked by the opposition and bring it back into play nearer to the opponent's try line. Unless we define all the roles in play, the game will be a mess, and none of the players will know which areas to cover. As a result, assumptions will be made, with some areas getting too much attention, and some none at all.

Key Performance Indicators

Once we've defined what the roles of each player are (what they are responsible for), each role should have some key measurables which they are personally answerable for, and that they can assess and improve (that they are accountable to). When this is clear, they can take ownership of that role and its improvement.

Let's continue with the examples used above. One of the hooker's key measures of performance would be how straight and accurately they feed the ball into the line-out. The full-back needs to be able to catch the ball one hundred per cent of the time and drop kick accurately over as long a distance as possible. These would represent their key areas of focus in the game.

By measuring these areas, they would know if they were performing well in the game, and which areas they needed to improve to raise the quality of their contribution. It's their measure to both assess their performance and develop.

How-to Manuals

Of course, it's all very well giving each player a clear definition of their role, and their key measures but, if they don't know the rules of rugby, there would be little point. In my example, the how-to manual would be the Rugby Football Union's rule book. If they don't know the system of play that they should be following, chances are the game won't hang together very well. Rules will be broken, and players would take it personally when the referee called them out on their behaviour. When the rules are clear, the referee's decisions become objective.

Remember this simple adage: the systems run the business and the people run the systems.

Management Systems

For every game, we need to keep score. If we don't, how do we know how many points we need to score to win? In my example, we'd also need to measure league performance, world rankings, etc.

While we'd need to meet as a team to keep innovating our game, we'd also need to coach and manage each player to improve their own performance, in order to elevate the overall performance of the team and achieve the game strategy.

Those measurement systems and the accountability loop to

examine performance, and define actions to improve that performance, are central to the development of the team.

SUMMARY

There, in brief, are the nine elements which contribute to a great game of rugby. Let me then get you to consider two questions:

If we removed any one of those nine key elements from the game, would it work as well? The answer is obviously a resounding "no". Given this:

Why would the game of business be any different?

If that's the case, then I guess we should examine each of the nine elements in a bit more detail in relation to business and get really clear on why they are important.

Now you're thinking smarter and doing less, this is the last piece of the jigsaw for you to get more from your business and your life.

Section 3: Getting MORE From Your Business and Your Life

Introduction

In the first two sections, we covered the principles you need to embrace to think smarter and do less. You should now be thinking bigger about where you want to go and focusing more on high-value activities.

This section is about achieving that elusive life and business freedom that most of us go into business to achieve, and then lose sight of as we progress on our business journey.

To achieve that freedom, there are a couple of qualifying criteria. First, it not only needs to be you that is embracing the principles we've talked about so far. Your team need to be thinking in the same way too. If you haven't already, teach them the principles from Section 1: Thinking Smarter. These form part of the systems in your business: the acceptable performance standards to which you can objectively hold people accountable.

Second, we've seen, in the previous chapter, that if we're going to play the game of business well, then we need to have implemented those nine key elements to create the systems of leadership and management. In other words, a clear framework for where we are going, how we're going to get there, and how each team member is involved in that journey.

Let's look then at the importance of each of those nine ways and talk more about their implementation into your business.

Chapter 6

Implementing the Nine Ways to Business Freedom: A Practical Roadmap

INTRODUCTION

There are two sides to the nine ways "equation". One side is leadership and the other side is management, and we need to make sure both sides are balanced as we saw in the previous chapter.

Leadership is about creation of alignment and engagement in your team. It's about getting them on the same page as you and behaving in the way you'd like them to. Essentially, it creates the "why" for people to understand the reason they are being managed.

When we come to the management part of this chapter, we'll delve into some of the tools you can implement to create the accountability you'll need. These will not only provide you with more accountability for you and your team, but a level of information which will give you the confidence that your business is running as you would like, whether you are there or not.

By the end of this chapter, you should be able to create the environment that allows you to experience that life and business freedom which so many covet!

But before we get stuck in, I think it may be useful to consider why the balance between leadership and management is so vital to you in achieving both success and business freedom. I tend to use a diagram for this.

The Balance of Leadership and Management

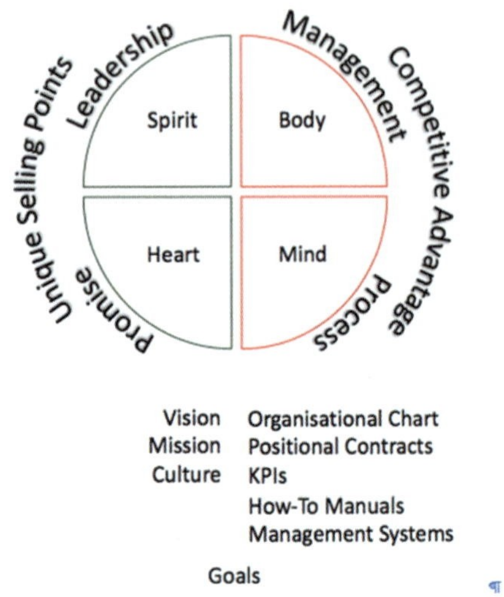

Figure 6.1: The nine ways of systematising a business

You'll notice in the diagram above that it's split into four quadrants. These are the four components which make up a person: physical intelligence (body), intellectual intelligence (mind), emotional intelligence (heart) and spiritual conscience (spirit). Stephen R. Covey talks about this at length in his seminal book on leadership, *The 8th Habit*[1]. I've split the nine ways and placed them under the side to which, in my opinion, they relate.

You'll also notice that I've labelled the body and mind side of the diagram as management and process. The heart and spirit side represent leadership and promise.

Let's consider for a moment the way markets have evolved. Go back to the agricultural revolution. One big landowner told lots of people what to do. Only the "body" element was required from an employee, as they just needed to turn up and dig a hole (or the equivalent).

---

[1] *The 8th Habit: From Effectiveness to Greatness,* Stephen R. Covey, Simon & Schuster, Jan 2006

Next came the industrial revolution. One big factory owner told lots of employees to "press that button one hundred times today" and they were done. In the main, only the body was needed again. At this time, there was little choice in the marketplace. For example, if you wanted a car, you had to have a Ford and you could have any colour you wanted as long as it was black!

We then moved into the technology age. Here, both mind and body were needed, as the jobs being performed were more complex – programming computers and the like.

In my opinion, we are now in the experience age. If you think about it, markets have fragmented to a large degree. There are many different variants of products out there and, for the most part, the differences are subtle. However, what *does* help us differentiate between them is our experience of the product or service. For example, if you have ever bought an Apple computer from the Apple shop, the experience of buying and unboxing the product will be entirely different to buying a Dell computer via their website. Though the products are ostensibly the same, the experience drives our perception of the product, as that's the part we really understand.

Think about this for a moment. What creates that experience for us? Of course, it's backed up by a process which ensures the consistency of the experience, but the experience itself is borne of the company's vision of who it wants to be in the marketplace, and the culture of how it wants to behave in that market.

In other words, the engagement of all four parts of a team member (body, mind, heart and spirit) becomes of paramount importance in the market environment in which we find ourselves today.

It's the vision, mission and culture which create alignment and engagement in the team. Those are the aspects which engage and inspire, and which create the recipe of values and behaviours that the team take to the marketplace. These are the aspects which distinguish your company and provide your unique selling points, or your recipe. We therefore need team members who *care* about how we want to present ourselves to the marketplace; in other words, people who are committed to fulfilling our brand promise.

The components of the leadership side of the equation are about emotional involvement.

On the right side of the diagram are the management and process aspects. Our process must follow our promise and thus our systems are designed to ensure that this promise is delivered consistently to the market, so they get what they expect. On this side of the circle, competitive advantage can be generated. This is where we have the opportunity to develop our processes to deliver our product or service in a different way: quicker, more efficiently, at higher margin or lower cost, for example. This may also help reinforce our promise.

As such, then, the leadership side of the diagram is vital to ensuring people are aligned with the direction of the business and are behaving in a way which reinforces the company's promises to the marketplace. The management side, on the other hand, ensures that the product or service gets into its customers hands as they expect, on a consistent basis.

To achieve this level of performance, therefore, we need to engage not only people's bodies and minds, but also their hearts and spirits. They need to *care* about the customers they are serving in order to deliver the recipe of the business consistently.

The nine ways are designed to elicit that clarity and engagement, and then back it up with the processes to meet the promise. The absence of any of these nine elements will more than likely lead to disappointment and confusion from customers as, not only will they get inconsistency in the quality of the product or service, but also in their experience through the customer journey.

To summarise, if we want to have a business which allows us to do less so we can experience more life and business freedom, we must design a system where process follows promise, consistently.

Creating Alignment in Your Team

Let's first look again at the four aspects I categorised as the leadership elements: vision, mission, culture and goals.

In many of the businesses I've coached, rarely have these already existed in any documented format. If they do exist and I ask the question: "What do they say?", not only would the team have little or no idea, but rarely does the owner of the business either. It's one of those tasks that some people do because they've heard that they *should*, but without realising their real value, or bringing them to life in the business.

Perhaps, then, we'd better get clear on the purpose and value of them. Let me ask you a question.

If you took all the team members in your business right now, stood them in a room together and told them to close their eyes and then point north, what are the chances that they would all be pointing in the same direction? Probably zero!

Now, let's imagine that they were all linked together, each holding a rope, all of which were tied together at a central point, and you asked them to pull north while they had their eyes closed. Some may not even decide to pull as they may just think, "I don't know why I need to" and therefore not contribute. If they did, however, they'd probably all think they were on the right track, even though they'd likely be pulling in different directions. No doubt they'd all have the best intentions, *thinking* that they were pulling in the right direction but, in reality, progress would be severely hampered, wouldn't it?

This is the point of the first four elements – vision, mission, culture and goals. Let's tell everyone where north is and get them all facing in the same direction. We can call that alignment.

Let's also think about this in the context of hiring new people into the team. When you advertise for a new team member or interview them, do you show them your vision, mission and culture statements? If not, how do you expect to attract people who are on the same page as you? By that, I mean people who are excited by where you are going as a business and share your values.

How much easier would it be to lead a team of people who are all aligned in purpose and values? And how much more likely are they to understand *why* they need to be managed to help the business get to its destination faster?

The sad fact is that, in the vast majority of businesses I have worked with, there is little or no communication of any of these aspects.

What do you think is the correlation between this and the statement (which I hear very regularly): "People only come to work for the money. Why don't they care about the business as much as I do?"

Would it be fair to say that it's because you haven't told them why they should?

For many, I'm guessing the answer may be yes, so let's look at the four elements of leadership in more detail.

Vision: Your Guiding Light

The vision of your business is the guiding light. ActionCOACH's vision is: "World abundance through business re-education". When I first started to investigate the franchise in 2007, this was pretty much the first document I was shown, and I loved it. I needed to find out more, as I absolutely identified with the sentiment of it. It inspired me, it engaged me, and I could immediately see myself being a part of an organisation with that as its purpose.

Let's consider the statement for a moment though. When Brad, ActionCOACH's founder, was sitting in his back bedroom in Brisbane in 1993, that vision would have appeared like a pretty bold statement, wouldn't it? In 2020, 27 years later, we operate in over 90 countries and have over 1,500 coaches worldwide. We're still not there yet: not enough countries, and definitely not enough coaches. But we are on track.

If Brad hadn't set his vision on such a grand scale, how many business owners across the planet would have missed out on the help that we provide? The very sentiment of that vision statement *forces* us to think bigger. We *have* to ask more challenging questions. As a result, if we're truly enrolled in that vision, we must take action to move towards it; all of us - every single coach under the ActionCOACH banner. If we don't, we're not *on purpose*, meaning we're not taking action towards our reason for being.

What's the quality of your vision right now? You may not want to conquer the world, but let me get you to consider this:

How much do you believe that what you offer is up there with the best in the market? Hopefully, there's a pretty strong belief there, because that belief in yourself is normally a part of the reason that caused you to start a business in the first place! Next, would it be fair to say that, in your industry, there are a fair few people who aren't doing a particularly great job; who may even be doing your industry some damage through their quality of service or the way they behave? If it's like my industry, the answer must be "of course".

Isn't it therefore your *responsibility* to help more people to achieve a better quality of service and really understand *what "great" looks like* in your industry? Don't all those people who currently don't know about you, who are missing out on your great service, and having to put up with the second-rate service of your competition, *deserve* to experience first class?

If your answer to all of the above is "yes", then isn't it time to start thinking differently about your business? How big does it need to be to serve those people? I'm not saying you have to think on a global scale like Brad did (though it's clearly possible). It may be that you want to be the best in your town, county or country, etc. You decide. But the point here is: if we're not thinking about the fulfilment of our vision, then our day-to-day challenges may just feel too big and onerous to move forward, and we may end up as a mediocre version of who we could have been.

Why wouldn't you set a big vision? Why shouldn't it scare you? Remember the success formula in the first section of this book? We started with *dreams*. In the same way as I've encouraged you to dream about the life you want to have (even if you don't believe it possible yet), I'd encourage you to do the same with your business. Why shouldn't you? If you don't, no one else will.

This is one of the first things I ask clients to think about, especially if they already have a good business. The challenge of a good business is that it's normally not yet a great business. The owner has grown it to a size which fulfils the life that they want and, once they hit this point, they start to feel like they are on the treadmill. They stop being excited about new horizons. I've met with numerous owners and asked them where they want their business to be one year from now. When they tell me, I normally ask them something like: "So, on a scale of 1 to 10, how excited are you about that?" The answer is normally low to middle. My next question is: "If that's how excited you are about it, how excited do you think your team are?"

Consider this in your business right now. How excited are you about where you are heading? Do you even know? And, if you don't, what chance do your team have? If this is the case, then the chances are you're on a collision course with burn out: the point at which you simply turn around and say to yourself, "I don't have the energy for this anymore".

Perhaps it's time to start thinking bigger. What about if you thought about a business that was *bigger than self*? By that, I mean a business that not only serves your lifestyle, but also serves the community in some way (however you may define community).

What I'm really talking about is your why: the reason that you were put on the planet. When I was growing up, I knew that I didn't want the quality of life that I had been given, so I realised that *I* had to transform it. Along the way I found that, as I transformed my life, I started to help others transform theirs too. When I look back on my life, there's evidence of this purpose scattered throughout it; not just inside work, but outside as well. This purpose defines me. The more people I help to transform their lives, the more authentic I feel.

What's your purpose? For most people, it comes back to service at some level. Deep down, we all need to feel like we belong and contribute: that's why it's not enough to just fulfil our own ends. It doesn't matter if you want to meet the needs of the world, or just your family, but your purpose is never about you!

If you start to think about what gets you out of bed in the morning, the things that really excite and drive you, then you're probably starting to get pretty close to your purpose. What would your business need to be like to live that?

This may all sound a bit pie in the sky but, if we look back over some of the research in this area, the clues have existed for years and years. A great example would be Maslow, who talked about a hierarchy of needs. At the bottom level were physiological needs, our basic requirements of food, water, warmth and rest; that is, the basics of keeping us alive. Next come safety and shelter, the things that start to give us a bit more comfort.

We then move to psychological needs. At this third level of his pyramid, he talks about belonging and love, the aspects that start to bring some meaning to our lives. Next comes esteem needs: the feeling of accomplishment and pride that starts to bring some fulfilment to our lives.

At the top level of his five-tier pyramid, he talks about self-actualisation: the fulfilment of one's potential. This is always *bigger than self.* It always involves contribution and service. It's about our why.

Why wouldn't you define the vision of your business to reflect your why? When I talk to potential new team members, I talk about my why. I tell them where we're going as a business, because it's connected to my why: I want to help as many people as possible transform their life beyond what they thought was possible. And, critically, I want people with me on my team who share my purpose and want to do the same.

When I look at the vision statements my clients have created, they are all about service and contribution. They are all about creating something bigger than themselves. With that comes emotion, and emotion is the reason we buy something, isn't it? Why would you *not* want your team members and clients (and prospective employees and customers) to have an emotional connection to your business? What if they were all engaged and inspired by the journey you want to go on? What if they had this purpose lodged in their mind so that they were thinking about how to help you get there?

A vision is a powerful thing. It makes the obstacles in our way appear small. It inspires us on a daily basis.

In my mind, there's a difference between motivation and inspiration. Motivation can be externally applied and is normally transient; it comes and goes. As such, it's difficult to be motivated all the time and, when we're not motivated, we're rarely moving forward. Motivation is normally enough to get us to move away from pain. It's the thing that causes us to do "just enough". The large majority of humans will settle for ordinary because they're motivated to get just enough to meet their needs.

Inspiration, on the other hand, tends to be a permanent, inner force. As opposed to motivation, which moves us away from pain, inspiration pulls us strongly towards pleasure, because we're emotionally connected to the feeling that we'll experience as we go there, whether that be pride, or recognition or, in other words, self-actualisation.

In essence, then, the reason that most people achieve at the level they do is due to lack of inspiration. As a result, they only ever do just enough to get them away from pain and then they stop as they're now comfortable again. But, if that's how we choose to behave, we are never far from pain. When we lose a big client, for example, it can drop us back into pain as we now don't have enough profit and/or cashflow in the business for it not to matter.

When you have a vision, in contrast, you will keep getting better and better, because you will constantly have to learn new things and improve to reach your goals; And your team will have to do the same.

Remember the equation we talked about earlier: "be" x "do" = "have". Your vision is your ultimate "have". How much will you and your team have to learn to get there? How will you have to think and act differently?

Very early on, we talked about the formula for success: dream x goal x learn x plan x act = success. Your vision statement is the dream for your business! When you set it, in the very same way that when you set your personal dreams, you shouldn't constrain it with the parameters of your current paradigm.

Set it high! Go big! Be brave! After all, the bigger you think, the bigger your team will have to think. And, let's face it, they're there to help you achieve your vision. You don't have to work it all out for yourself!

Let's work through a real client example.

Here's the final version of their vision:

"To revolutionise the building materials market by becoming the UK's first choice company for building projects".

But it didn't start there. This is the first attempt:

> "To transform the way building materials are sold online and become the number one company for flat roof systems".

That's a pretty good vision in itself. The company was created to sell roofing systems online, in a more consumer-friendly way. This led to the development of systems to help the consumer specify their project right, first time, and end up with all of the constituent elements they needed to complete the project. The vision was therefore borne out of frustration that consumers couldn't easily buy what they needed to do a roofing project.

When we began to discuss the vision with the team, the final evolution appeared. It was about not only the market sector that this particular business existed in, but also the much wider building materials market. Through our discussions, the possibilities for the business expanded dramatically, as they realised that the ideas that they were already executing in one area were transferrable to other markets.

If we really pull apart what's gone on here, we can see how we got to this vision. The original draft was driven by a core value: that consumers should be educated enough to specify projects for themselves without being frustrated or exploited. The values were fairness, integrity and transparency, which have been reflected in the final vision and in how they are starting to serve the marketplace.

If you think about what really frustrates you about the market that you operate in, it will probably be something which clashes with your values in some way or another. Take that frustration and harness it in your vision to address this. If you are frustrated by it, I can guarantee that there are plenty of others out there who'll be frustrated by it too, both as potential team members and as customers. Unite them under your vision and you will have a powerful vehicle.

Write a vision statement for your business. It doesn't have to be the final version, but it should be something that inspires you. It also doesn't have to be long. It could simply be: "To be the number one in a chosen location".

How does that cause you to start thinking differently? And, when you share it with your team, how will it cause them to start thinking differently too?

Mission: Your Roadmap to the Destination

Your mission statement is the roadmap to your vision. In it, you start to flesh out what's important on your journey: the business you are in, who your customers are, what makes you different and what your key characteristics are. It is the next level in your playbook.

Let's continue with the example from above, as it delivers the expansion of the idea really well. Here is their mission statement:

> *"The buying and selling of building materials as individual items that require manual calculations will be a thing of the past.*
>
> *Manufacturers will be queueing up to take advantage of a more direct, simpler, leaner way of quoting and delivering project-based building materials.*
>
> *Customers will finally have the ability to create quotations and make informed decisions that will save time and money thanks to a new standardised way of selling that provides the knowledge required to choose the correct system for their project.*
>
> *Competitors will either have become part of our supply network or lost their leading market share.*
>
> *The transformation of the flat-roofing marketplace will have set the benchmark for us in taking on the wider construction industry."*

As you can see, this expands on the vision of the business, and starts to set out the component parts. It deals with customers, suppliers and the marketplace as a whole, and it's easy to see that, if all of these elements were successfully addressed, the business would be well on track towards its vision's end goal.

As a result, it now becomes much easier to ask more pertinent questions about what strategies need to be deployed to move the business forward.

Write the mission statement for your business, considering these four questions:

1. Who are we?
2. What business are we in?
3. Who are our customers?
4. What makes us unique?

Culture: The Bedrock of Your Business Recipe

I can't stress the importance of culture enough. It forms the foundations for the behaviour which will define you in the marketplace you serve. The problem in many organisations is that the culture doesn't always serve the company well; Usually, the main reason is that the culture has not been built deliberately, but has evolved, over time, based on what people deem to be acceptable.

In his book, *The Advantage*[2], Patrick Lencioni talks about four types of culture or values in an organisation. I really empathise with his definitions and use them regularly with clients. These are:

- Core values
- Permission to play values
- Aspirational values; and
- Accidental values

---

[2] *The Advantage: Why Organizational Health Trumps Everything Else In Business,* Patrick M. Lencioni, Jossey-Bass, April 2012

Let's look at each, in turn, and consider the impact on your business.

Core Values

These are the values which define the business; those which someone, when looking from the outside in, would refer to by saying: "They're the guys who....". The customer will speak of the values they perceive to be the defining characteristics of your organisation. In figure 6.1, we showed that the core values of the business can be the thing that help to define its uniqueness, as this "recipe" forms the basis of the customer experience.

When you started your business, your clients probably came to you because they liked the way you served them. I call that your "recipe": your unique mix of ingredients which makes your clients want to do business with you.

Clearly, as we are growing our business, we need to employ people to create leverage and scalability. We therefore need to systematise our recipe, as we want our clients to have the same experience whether they deal with us personally or not. Otherwise, we'll either be forever tied to the business and limited in the scale we can achieve, or delivering inconsistent (and therefore undefinable and confusing) experiences to our clients.

Normally, there are four or five core values in an organisation. When you recruit, you should question people around these values to ensure that they are present in your potential new team member. Why would you want to recruit someone who didn't share your values? After all, it's much easier to lead and manage team members who are aligned with your vision, mission and culture. As Tony Hsieh (founder of Zappos shoe store, an online business founded in 1999 and sold to Amazon in 2009 for $940 million) states: "If you get the culture right, most of the other stuff will just take care of itself".

Your core values are the bedrock of the behavioural expectations for your team. They have to be written down (they're part of your system), clearly explained and discussed regularly to ensure they "live" in your business.

How do you define your core values? Most people find it

difficult to articulate their values, so it's sometimes easier to just look at what really frustrates or upsets us. Those are the things that are really in opposition to our values (go back to the definition of values from the identity iceberg: values are the things which are *important* to us). For example, if it frustrates you when people are rude to you when you are driving, then politeness is probably one of your values. If you get angry when people are treated unfairly, then you probably believe that everyone should have the same opportunities, and equality would be a value. It's your job to pin down your most important values, the ones which you feel truly define you, and thus the service you want to offer to the world. That mixture of values will form your recipe.

You may have identified some of my values as you read this book, but let me explain them more fully so you can see how everything fits together. I have three core values:

- Personal development
- Balance
- Resilience

When I look at how these values play out in my life, it's completely clear to me why I have this business and structure it in the way that I do. You see, I am continuously on a journey to learn more. When I learn more, I can perform better as I think differently. I guess you could call that "thinking smarter". I'm also committed to getting balance in my life between business, family and myself; Hence I only choose to work three days per week (let's call that "doing less"). But I also know that to get to a point where I'm performing at a high level in order to achieve this takes time, and I'll take some knock backs. That's fine, but I will *never* give up (resilience). So, there are my three values explained. When I start thinking about how those values show up in my working life, I can see I've created a time-leveraged business which helps people become better and get their lives back. That, in turn, creates the foundation for my vision to help all the business owners in my community be better, achieve more and gain the freedom they deserve from their businesses.

Thus, as you start to get clear on your core values, your vision will become obvious, and you'll find examples of them both running through your whole life!

If those values are so important that they form the basis of your vision, they will also impact on how you take your product or service to market (your customer experience). We should definitely, therefore, make sure that the people on our team share those values.

Either:
Make a list of the things that really annoy you. What value is that reflecting back to you?

Or:
List your core values; that is the four or five values which make up your "recipe", the reason why your customers buy from you.

Or:
Survey your top customers and ask them for the top five words to describe their experience of doing business with you. Identify the words which show up most often.

I do a fascinating exercise with clients: I get them to list their core values across the top of a piece of paper, and then their team members down the side. Then I get them to "set the bar". This means they need to decide what the acceptable level of performance is against these values. They can score red (the behaviours indicating this value is never demonstrated), amber (sometimes demonstrated) or green (always demonstrated). Obviously, no reds are allowed when they set the bar, but they decide for each of the values whether they should be green or amber. The "bar" needs to be set prior to thinking about specific members of the team. Next, they take a set of red, amber and green pens and mark up, for each team member, what level they reach against each value.

I've conducted this exercise many times and, without exception, the people who have scored red anywhere have ended up leaving the business.

The point is this: why would you want people on your team who are not aligned with your values? Especially your core values which are, by their very nature, the ones which define you.

The value of this exercise is that it now gives you an *objective* way to analyse your team. Prior to doing this, I've found that most clients have had a feeling for which members of their team are right and which aren't, but this has helped them to explain that feeling more easily.

Perform a "set the bar" exercise for your team now. What did you learn?

Permission to Play and Aspirational Values

Lencioni then talks about "permission to play" values: those which should exist within a team member in order to be a part of your team (let's use honesty as an example). Everyone should exhibit the value, but they're not the values which define you. Nevertheless, when you recruit a new team member, you should interview to ensure that the value is present.

The third type are aspirational values: hose which you would *like* your team to display, but which they don't yet do so consistently. Let's take the value of curiosity as an example. It may be important to you that your team become curious about your customers' needs in order that they may provide a better service to them. This may not be a core value, and you may already have a great product or service. Curious becomes the "icing on the cake" and therefore needs to become an active element of your culture.

You've already created a list of your core values. Now list the permission to play, and aspirational values for your business.

Congratulations! You now have a culture statement. All you need to do now is clearly define the behaviours that you deem exhibit each value and embed them in the business. The question is: how?

Before we talk about how to do that, we should mention the fourth type of value that Lencioni describes. These are the embodiment of the culture that has built itself, and they are:

Accidental Values

Accidental values are the things which have become "the way things are done around here". They have arisen by accident and, through lack of consciously and proactively building a culture, they haven't been put in check.

For example, years ago I worked with a client whose team were allowed a 15-minute break in the morning and afternoon. The original idea was that they reach a convenient stopping point and take their break. For a while, this all worked perfectly, and the team were efficient and chose their break times sensibly. A new team member then joined the business, who insisted on taking her break at 10.15am, without fail, even if still in the middle of a task. Over time, one became two, two became three, and three became many. As a result, a "work to rule" type attitude grew within the business where, at 10.15am precisely, the business ground to a halt! How much wasted time and inefficiency did that one single act introduce into that business?

The point is this: if you don't actively build your culture, then your team will build it for you. And, unfortunately, they may not build the one you want. They'll bring elements of their previous experience to your business, and what will result is an amalgam of lots of different values and ideas which don't necessarily convey how you want your business to be thought of.

How much of this accidental behaviour do you see in your business right now? More importantly, whose fault is that?

Building Your Culture

Let's go back to implementation.

I've had the privilege of hearing Sir Clive Woodward speak on a couple of occasions. He talks about his experiences of building a culture in both the 1993 World Cup-winning English rugby team, and in the Olympic team. He employs the idea of "teamship". In essence, he gets the team to create and deploy the culture. And you can do the same. Now you have your list, why not get your team to develop the meanings for you?

Ultimately, you'll sign their ideas off once they have agreed upon the definitions, so you still have overall control of the direction of travel. It's then their job to make the culture "live" in your business.

I have a client who has a "word of the week" where each week's word describes the intended culture. It's the team's job to discuss the word, find evidence of it being played out in the business and then talk about it.

What we're really talking about here is stories, and we all know that stories bring things to life, make them accessible and provide fuel for new ideas.

What stories are being created around the culture in your business right now?

Goals: The Bridge Between Leadership and Management

We've already talked in detail about goals, so I don't intend to expand further here.

By now, however, it should be abundantly clear how the idea of goals fits into the overall strategic alignment of your team. If vision is the final destination, then goals are the objective waymarkers to ensure that you are on track.

When you've completed the tasks above, you'll have a clear set of statements in your business which you now have to bring to life. The only way to do that is to talk about them *frequently* and, let's be fair, why wouldn't you? These are, after all, the guiding principles of your business. We now have the "recipe" to take out to the marketplace and provide a clearly articulated *promise*; that is, the customer experience that our current and prospective clients should be educated to expect.

Let's now expand on the five other elements of the nine areas. It's great to have your *promise* but now you need a *process*, because process follows promise. In other words, we need to deliver what we say we are going to deliver.

Organisational Chart: Your Play Sheet

Most businesses I work with don't have an organisational chart in place, either for the business in its current shape, or the business in its finished format.

What do I mean by that? When we start our business, the team normally consists of one person. As a consequence of that, we are responsible for every role. As we grow and hire people, we pass some of our roles to other people. That's leverage: dividing to multiply in order to create more time for people to specialise and play to their strengths more of the time. In reality, though, the tasks which get passed over aren't always done by design. Instead, they are just passed to other people because they are there. In other words, the specific roles required to enable the business to function efficiently aren't designed into the business. Instead, jobs are simply passed to people to do.

In many of the businesses I work with, the MD is still wearing a lot of hats. They are the MD (though how long they actually spend operating in that position is up for debate), and they may also still have a hand in the operational aspects of the business, be responsible for business development, and the list goes on.

Because in many businesses there are numerous people doing numerous roles, it's sometimes difficult to separate everything out so it makes sense. We tend to think about people, not roles. As a result, people normally have some areas of responsibility which make sense for them, and some which absolutely do not. When we think purely in terms of people in the business, it's like looking at a big ball of tangled spaghetti.

I therefore encourage clients to draw an organisational chart that reflects a point in the future rather than the current situation. It might be the point at which they exit the business, or it may be at the point they achieve their one-year goals. Either way, the question I'm really getting them to think about is: what are the roles that need to exist in the business to achieve that goal or the end in mind?

By simply drawing out an organisational chart, it not only gives us clarity of the separate roles in the business, but also allows us to put a rough budget on what that business would cost to resource if we were to employ those separate roles. Normally this exercise in itself creates an inordinate amount of clarity, along with realisations that there are plenty of people in the business doing stuff which doesn't make sense in relation to the rate they are being paid at (and that almost always includes the MD!)

We can relate this directly back to the orange box idea we discussed earlier (see figure 4.6). As we begin to map out the tasks everyone is doing, it's normally easy to see where the lower-value tasks are being carried out. As a result, it's possible to define the role required to do those tasks in order to allow the more highly-skilled members of the team to focus on their higher-value tasks more of the time.

To give you an example, I worked with a client where the MD insisted on entering the purchase invoices on to the accounting system. That's a £10 per hour job, at best, and this was a business with a £10 million turnover! Just how many purchase invoices do you think there were in that business and, as a consequence, what proportion of the week was the MD spending working at an hourly rate of £10? Back to that scarcity thinking where we believe it doesn't make sense to hire someone new whereas, in reality, it doesn't make sense not to. For the princely sum of £200 per week, we hired someone to free up well over a day a week of the MD's time. This meant he could now manage the sales team, which he clearly couldn't do before as he was too busy processing purchase invoices! The real point here is that there are many low-value tasks in every business and, if we get clear on what they are and then design a role to undertake them, it's rarely a huge expense to remove them from the equation. Ultimately, the opportunity cost of freeing up a skilled person's time to spend more at their hourly rate has never failed to pay back that investment.

Pick a point in the future in relation to one of the important goals you have defined, or think about the structure of your business when you finally reach the finish line (i.e. the point at which you exit).

Draw the organisational chart for this point in time. Next, allocate a rough budget to each position.

Positional Contracts: The Key to "a Great Day"

We've already mentioned that positional contracts are concise documents which outline a team member's specific responsibilities in your business. In other words, we're answering the question: "What does a great day look like?"

A positional contract should contain four key areas:

- Duties and responsibilities
- Results or expectations
- Performance standards; and
- Skills and abilities

It also lists who the role reports to, the hours, pay grade and probation period. A positional contract is normally a one-page document; it's about creating focus and clarity, so it should be brief.

Let's look at each of those areas in turn.

- Duties and responsibilities. This should be a list of the responsibilities relating to the role. Effectively, these are the orange box activities which should be mapped onto the team member's default diary (as these are their priorities, and we must always schedule our priorities). Ideally, each team member should have around five or six responsibilities and no more.

- Results or expectations. These are the specific deliverables that the team member is expected to attain. In other words, key performance indicators, which we'll cover next.

- Performance standards: These are the behavioural criteria, for example, that the team member should adhere to. Examples might be that phone calls should be answered within three rings, or that timesheets should be completed and submitted daily.

- Skills and abilities. These are the role-specific skills which the team member should already possess or be in the process of acquiring.

Here's an example of a positional contract (figure 6.2). In it, you'll see the key activities and skills required to fulfil the role of "Relationship Development Manager" in my business. I can now hold the person in that role accountable to the orange box items defined in the duties and responsibilities section and I have defined the reporting requirements and expectations in the performance standards section.

Figure 6.2: Positional contract example

ActionCOACH

Position Contract

Agreement to fulfill the accountabilities of the job

Position Title: Relationship Development Manager		
Location: Office based with necessary territory visits		
Line manager: Andy Hemming **Title: MD**		
Pay Rate: £xx FTE plus bonuses **Probationary Period: 3 months** **Performance Review Date:**	**Type of position:** **☐ Full-time** **x Part-time** **☐ Contractor** **☐ Apprentice** **☐ Work experience**	**Hours of work:** **25 / week, flexible to suit needs of role**

My duties and responsibilities in this position are:

1. Make noise in the territory by building both 1 to 1 and strategic relationships.
2. Represent the company in the Black Country area at selected network events (e.g. Black Country Chamber of Commerce) to meet business owners, develop relationships and educate regarding the possibilities in coaching.
3. Grow and nurture the database of qualified business owners (i.e. people who have met us face to face and are interested in continuing a conversation at some level) through appropriate communication.
4. Identify, build and maintain relationships with potential strategic alliances (e.g. banks, accountants, solicitors) in order to create speaking and referral opportunities
5. Develop group offerings such as book club, profit club and facilitate these sessions (i.e. coach the attendees)
6. Develop the quarterly plan in conjunction with all team members

I will achieve the following results in this position:

1. Identify and attend appropriate networking events in the territory.
2. Increase the number of prospects on the database by 20 per week
3. Generate at least 1 qualified appointment per week with prospects in target market for 121 coaching
4. Generate 1 strategic alliance event per month – work with strategic partners to help them fill and deliver events, ensuring that all attendees are contacted, nurtured and followed up.
5. Measure and record activity on weekly dashboard to facilitate ongoing improvement in results

I will meet these standards while working in this position:

- Be flexible, committed and adaptable to do whatever it takes to move towards the vision of the business
- Play by the rules of the game
- Commit to continuous personal development (all learning materials provided)

I already have or will quickly develop the following knowledge, skills and abilities needed for this position:

- Excellent written and verbal communication skills and a great sense of humour
- High levels of resilience and determination
- An excellent understanding of the market and our coaching solutions

I will start work on / This Position Contract is effective from: [date]

Let's say that you now create a positional contract for each of the roles on your organisational chart. When you have this in place, what happens to your level of clarity about your business?

First, it's now easy to see where time is being consumed in low-value activities by people being paid too much to do them. Redeploy those tasks or hire someone else to do them.

Second, the orange box items for the business are now clear, so they can be mapped onto someone's default diary to ensure that they happen. Right now, there are probably a number of important balls being dropped or not given enough focus.

Third, it's easy to see *who* needs to be hired to alleviate bottlenecks in the business. Often, this exercise makes it very obvious how much extra valuable time can be freed up in the days of more highly skilled people if someone was recruited at a lower rate of pay to take up these tasks.

Fourth, it allows you to separate roles from people, thereby introducing a more objective view of the business. In its simplest form, it allows you to see how many hats you're wearing.

Write a positional contract for each of the roles you defined on the organisational chart.

Key Performance Indicators: The Link From Behaviour to Performance

What gets measured gets managed. We've all heard that adage before, yet I never fail to be surprised by how little actually does get measured in businesses.

Each team member should have at least a couple of measurable performance indicators. Of course, they need to be used in the correct way; they are absolutely not a stick to beat them with. We need each team member to take ownership of their contribution to performance. So, the first step is to define the areas which they need to measure, and then to get the measurement. Whatever that turns out to be, it's your baseline, and it represents an opportunity for improvement, not judgement!

Each team member should be focused on their KPIs, to the extent that they are constantly thinking about how to improve them. To make that happen, we need to measure regularly. In the absence of consistent and regular measurement, we tend to find that slippage happens. Let me give you an example. I weigh myself every day. The reason I do that is because change happens so incrementally that, if I don't weigh myself for a week or so, I don't *see* any change in my appearance, so I don't think anything has changed. If, after a month, I jump on the scales, the normal reaction is one of shock! How did that happen? I didn't catch the slippage (incremental weight increase) because I was making a subjective judgement on what I saw in the mirror rather that what the actual, objective number was on the scales. The only way to know if we are achieving consistency or improvement is to measure regularly and objectively and keep a record so we can compare results to establish a trend.

Of course, in the above example, I have full ownership for what exercise I do and what I eat and drink, but I can't think about the adjustments I need to make unless I know what the impact is. Your team members need to have the same level of ownership. If someone turned around to me and said, "Look at your weight! That's too much!", I'd probably characterise that as a "stick". I wouldn't be motivated and I'm very unlikely to get into a positive mindset about change. Instead, I'd probably get really defensive and grab a biscuit.

Conversely, someone could ask me questions like:

- What's your current weight?
- What would you like it to be?
- What one thing could you do in the next week which could make a difference to that number?

I'd be more willing to take ownership and come up with a plan to get there. It's really important to encourage that culture of ownership and innovation in your team members, or you'll forever tie yourself to being the only person who will come up with ideas to improve performance, which your team may (or may not) buy into. There's only one word for that: exhausting!

To determine relevant KPIs, it's worth sitting down with each of your team members and having a sensible discussion, based around their positional contract, to discover what they perceive their KPIs to be. There are obviously two elements to this: the activity and the result.

For example, when I employed telemarketers in my business, the numbers were as follows: 100 dials generated 16 conversations with decision makers which, in turn, generated one meeting. By knowing those numbers, we were able to set an activity expectation (100 dials per day) and an expected outcome (16 conversations and one appointment). Of course, the outcome of one appointment per day was the important measure. If the team member could generate a meeting with less than 100 dials, then that was a great result. By measuring those numbers every day, we could see how each team member was performing and then adjust the training required based on where the numbers weren't working as expected. Of course, if the team member was only doing 60 dials per day and not generating a meeting, it was an activity problem and not a system problem, so it also helped us to determine the cause.

Each team member should therefore have at least one meaningful performance indicator to measure and focus on, being a combination of desired outcome and predicted activity to achieve that outcome.

Meet with each of your team members and agree at least one performance indicator which aligns them with their part in achieving the results you want in your business. They should be outcome-based, and also include a measure of activity.

How-to Manuals: Your Route to Delegation

I've already mentioned the concept that systems run the business and people run the systems.

Many ignore the importance of systems (and, by systems, I mean *written* documents detailing how a task should be performed, as discussed in Chapter 5).

Let's explore this now.

When I start working with many of my clients, there are either few or no systems and processes documented. What does that mean? In reality, it means that you don't own your systems. Because, logically, if you haven't created and taught your system to your team, then one of two things will happen: either they have created a process of their own or, when you recruited them, they bought someone else's process with them and implemented it into your business.

But, let's remember, we're attempting to make process follow promise. If your team aren't applying *your* system, what are the chances that they may be missing some fairly important parts of your recipe? As a result, process may not follow your promise, and your clients will be either confused or receive inconsistent experiences when they deal with you.

The systems in your business should reflect the customer experience, the recipe, that you're looking to put out there into the marketplace. They should be *your* systems.

What's one of the best systems in the world? McDonald's. Consider the model for a moment. On average, the business is run by 24-year-olds and the team are made up of 16 to 17-years-old. The owner has to attend the business once per year because it's in their agreement. It produces the same consistent quality from restaurant to restaurant, and that's only because of the systems. Now, let's imagine that a McDonald's restaurant hires someone who has previously been working in KFC. No doubt they turn up for their first day at work, excited, wanting to do a great job. However, instead of teaching the new team member the McDonald's way, they just leave them to it. We now have a highly motivated employee running around the restaurant looking for chicken!

It's a silly example, I know. But, the reality is, this happens every single day in business. Was the team member ineffective when you hired them, or did you make them ineffective? Either way, you need to look to the system, either the recruitment system or the systems and processes which the team member should be operating (and part of that system is the training procedure).

Remember the rule about assessing where the problem lies in the business: system first, training second and person third. In the absence of systems and training, the wriggle room we talked about earlier exists in abundance. There's simply no way of making an objective judgement as to whether the team member is effective or not.

In order to make that decision objectively, systematise the process, train the team on the system and then measure the output. Wriggle room gone and consistency achieved!

But, most importantly, when we systematise to create measured, predictable consistency in our businesses, how much of a need is there for Superman? None!

It follows then that one of your key roles as MD of your business is to facilitate the creation of efficient and effective systems to create that predictable consistency. Create the rules to your game and document them, in whichever format you prefer: written, audio, video or a combination of all of the above.

We're not just talking about the systems for undertaking tasks, by the way. We also need to include the systems for measuring and reporting, and the systems for management. Of course, it's great to set up the systems, but we have to ensure that they are being adhered to; and that's management.

Wouldn't it be fantastic if we could tell someone once and then rely on them to internalise that process and implement it?

As I'm sure you've realised, though, life doesn't work like that! Chet Holmes, in his book, *The Ultimate Sales Machine*[3], sums this up beautifully:

"People respect what you inspect."

---

[3] *The Ultimate Sales Machine*, Chet Holmes, Penguin, 2007

Your system needs to include the inspection procedure, or I guarantee that slippage will happen, and your team will go back to their old ways.

Creating Your Systems

Often, when we think about creating the systems in our business, it appears a monumental task. To the extent, in fact, that many decide that it's just easier to continue to do it for themselves.

But who said that it was the business owner who had to create the systems? Sure, they have the overall ownership of the system, but they don't personally have to create them. In fact, in my opinion, if that's what they chose to do, they'd be missing the point.

You see, to move from a largely unstructured business to one which operates from its systems takes a fair amount of re-education of the team. Wouldn't it make sense for them to be involved in the creation of those systems, therefore, so that they not only understood how they work, but *why* they're being created?

Think about it. If your business is largely unsystematised, your team will be applying their own system, i.e. their personal way of doing things. They may have been taught it by another member of the team but, if it's not written down, I guarantee that they will have innovated their own process. By innovate, I mean they will have found a shortcut to get it done more quickly and efficiently for them. The problem with this is that, in so doing, they won't have taken into consideration the impact of the shortcuts they've implemented further down the process as it finds its way through the business into the hands of many different team members. In other words, they will do what's best for *them* and not what's best for the *business* as they only see the micro view and not the macro.

When we consider systematising the business, then, it's worth getting the team involved. I always show the whole team a fantastic nine minute video. It's a TED talk by Jim Wujec (go to www.drawtoast.com) about the process of making toast. Daft as that may sound, it's amazing that, when people are asked to draw the process of making toast, the output is vastly different. The big learning in this short talk is that even a very simple process that almost everyone knows how to undertake can be interpreted and conducted in a myriad of different ways.

When we add the complexity of the processes in our business, i.e. the multiple stages in the process, coupled with multiple transferences of responsibility as it travels through the organisation, then it's little wonder that so much confusion, duplication, error and inefficiency arises.

I'd recommend that you show this video to your team and then conduct the exercise for the key processes in your business. There are really only four of these at a macro level: marketing to create leads, sales to convert them, operations to deliver the job and finance to make sure that the cash cycle operates effectively and the margins are good.

Personally, I would always start with the delivery map, meaning the customer experience: the point at which the customer first contacts your business up until the moment the job is done. Of course, there are subsidiary processes to follow on from this as we need to stay in contact with the customer to get them to return and spend more with us. However, right now, let's just focus on getting everyone to have a consistent experience with us, and making sure it's one where they talk to people about it in a positive way.

By getting the team to help you define the processes, you automatically raise their level of knowledge as to how the business works, and they spot the inefficiencies, opportunities for improvement, duplications and holes. As a result of their conversations they will be able to re-engineer the process to make it far slicker and more robust, usually creating profit opportunities as a result.

I normally get teams to undertake the process in five steps:

1. Map the process from end to end using Post-It notes so they have flexibility to move ideas around and slot in any omissions, etc. One Post-it note per idea is the rule, as this means that the process flow can be rapidly iterated and re-engineered. The result is a long line of Post-Its which map the way that the process is currently performed. Usually, as a result of

this portion of the exercise, the team have massive learnings. They begin to see why the process flows as it does. They start to understand how everything moves through the business and they are able to make connections between what happens and how it could be done better.

2. As a result, they can now start to redesign the process, where necessary, to engineer out the duplications and inefficiencies. They can also build in more steps to make the process more customer-centric and provide more "wow" moments.

3. Next step is to assign responsibility. I get them to create horizontal lines relating to each function, department or role, as appropriate, and then simply move the Post-It notes to the right level. By breaking down the process into such small steps, it normally identifies simple tasks which can move to a lower pay rate in the business, freeing up the time of the higher earner to do more of the high-value tasks.

   The result is now the same process flow but allocated by responsibility in the business.

4. Next, determine the systems which are needed to support each of the steps in the process. For example, an inbound call may need a script for the person responsible to follow. Checklists may be required to ensure completeness. A video walkthrough may be necessary.

   The process is now becoming more robust as each of the stages is backed up by a specific method of undertaking it.

   Ensure that the controls are clear. By that I mean, when a process flows through a business, it normally moves between team members numerous times. At each point in the process, where responsibility transfers, put a control in place to ensure that the task has been done to the standard of the system. If not, then the task should be passed back as, if it were to continue further down the process, more error or inefficiency automatically becomes built in.

5. Design the measures. In other words, there will be a few key points in the process which will need to be measured and recorded in order to ensure that the process is operating consistently. Unless we create some performance indicators in the process, we have no way of identifying the slippage or areas of improvement we talked about earlier. Allocate these performance indicators to the person responsible for them to record and report.

Here's an example of a finished process flow (figure 6.3) showing the movement through the business, the systems required and the measurement steps:

Management Systems: The Route to Elevated Performance

You've probably noticed the word "objective" has cropped up a number of times lately. How many decisions do you think are made in businesses based on gut feel? (By the way, GUT = Gave Up Thinking).

As we've seen, instinct isn't enough. We need scoreboards to measure what we have to do to win. They set a target for performance and provide focus. It's the final part of the jigsaw to create an aligned, focused, engaged and responsive team.

But it's not enough to simply measure. We also need to manage. But be careful not to micromanage. If you've undertaken each of the previous steps, no micromanagement will be needed, as you will have a team of aligned members who know their place in your business and are clear on the systems they are expected to apply.

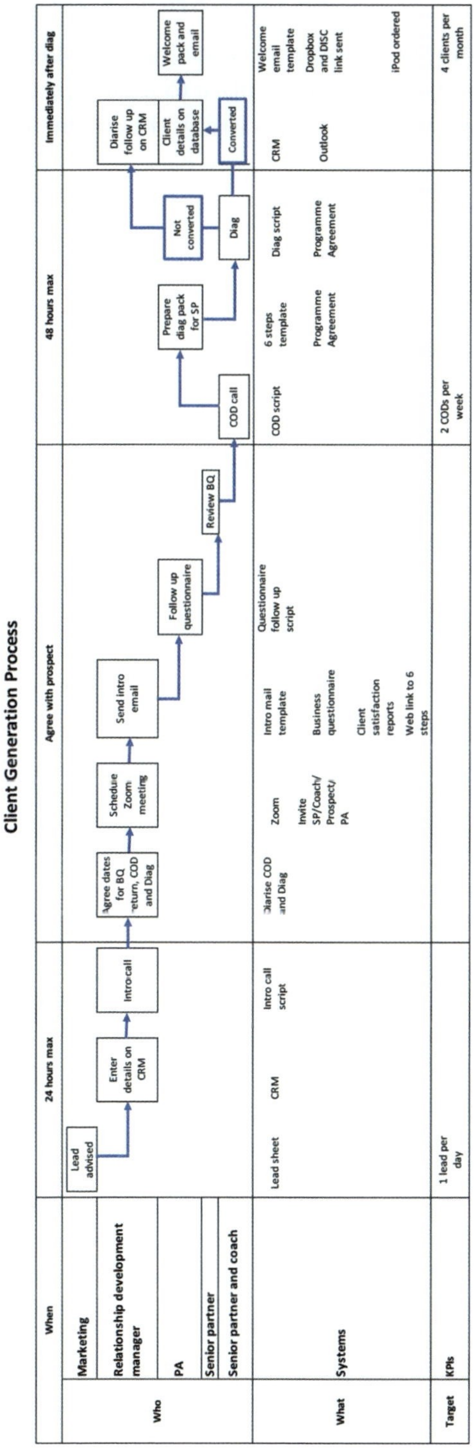

Figure 6.3: Sales process example

By management, I mean a systematic, objective accountability loop which challenges and supports the results of each member of the team; and that means a meeting. We call them "LION" meetings.

LION meetings

LION meetings are your vehicle for the creation of this accountability loop. LION is an acronym, and it's the simplest, yet most effective method of challenge and support for your team. It stands for:

L: Last week
I: Issues
O: Opportunities
N: Next week

These provide a quick and simple accountability and focus session.

Last week. Did you achieve what you said you were going to achieve?

Issues. What issues are arising for you right now? Is this a system issue or an exception? Do we need to do any training?

Opportunities. Where do you perceive the opportunities to be right now in your job?

Next week. What are you committing to achieve in the next week?

If you imagine sitting down for a one-to-one meeting at the same time every week with each of your key team members, and going through this format, just how much more accountability and focus would you have in your business right now? Notice I said that these meetings need to happen at the same time each week. Management is an orange box activity, and therefore should be a default diary entry. (Schedule your priorities!)

How long does that meeting need to be? In most cases, less than half an hour, per week. And, if each team member were to arrive with a report of their key performance indicators, you'd both be able to make an objective evaluation of whether what they were doing was working.

We therefore need to establish objective reporting procedures so that when we sit down to discuss performance, it is based on fact, not feeling. And, for that, we need to test and measure.

Test and Measure

Numbers are the language of business, and business is rooted in logic. Many of the business owners I meet are making too many decisions based on gut feeling and emotion. By their very nature, they are *subjective*, and this seriously reduces their quality. It also increases the fear factor, as it's easier to go into scarcity mentality such as, "I can't afford it", or, "I have to sell to everyone I get in front of", as a result.

Every game has a scoreboard of one type or another, and the game of business is no different. We have to put a number on everything and make the game objective. Then we will know what we need to do to win and can take the necessary actions to do so.

Think about it in the context of leverage. How many things could you measure in your business to save you time, save you money, or make you money?

Do you know the margin of everything you sell? If you haven't measured it, how do you know that you're making money on everything? My first client owned a car body repair shop. He was a fantastic guy with a great business which was making profit, and he had a great attitude to challenge and growth. When we pulled his numbers apart, we found that one of his customers (25% of his turnover) was actually costing him money. Not only that, they paid late to boot. After three months of "gentle persuasion" from me, he sacked them as a client, and immediately became more profitable! Three months later, they came back, accepting a 20% price increase. They then always paid to the 30-day deadline, by the way, as they couldn't get a service as good as his anywhere else.

If we hadn't known those numbers, we couldn't have taken that action. Imagine me suggesting that he go and reduce his turnover by 25% because I "thought" that this customer wasn't profitable. Or, indeed, that we hadn't found out at all and he just continued to serve them under the old arrangement.

By testing and measuring, we can make higher quality decisions and do more of the things that generate us money, and less of the things that don't: less is always more! But what do we need to measure? Let's consider that in some more detail.

Bubbles in Balance

In *The E-Myth Revisited*[4], Gerber talks about the three states a business owner falls into. He calls them technician, manager and entrepreneur. We've talked about this earlier to some extent.

An engineer sets up an engineering business and begins to work on the shop floor, making the widgets. That's the work of a technician: operational work. Rarely would you have to pay anyone more than £10-£15 per hour, at most, to do this kind of work. But they busy themselves with it anyway, because they are now making money. Capacity is limited by their available time, however, and eventually they'll hit the ceiling of their capacity.

While they're busying themselves with the operational work of the business, who is generating *new* business (the entrepreneur, taking care of sales and marketing)? And who is looking after the finances to make sure that the cashflow is protected (the manager)?

If we were to draw three bubbles with the sizes representing the amount of focus given to each of these areas, it would probably look something like figure 6.4.

If we're going to get to a business which is predictable and consistently growing, we absolutely need to focus on getting our bubbles in balance, i.e. a similar amount of focus being given to generating new work (sales and marketing), doing the work

---

[4] *The E-Myth Revisited: Why Most Small Businesses Don't Work and What to Do About It*, Michael E. Gerber, Harper Business, 2001

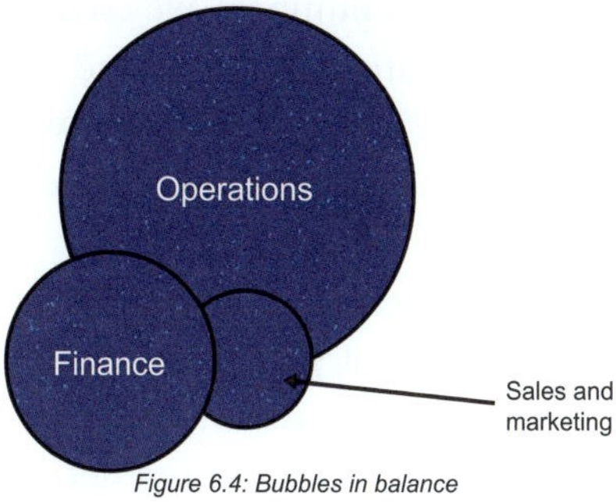

Figure 6.4: Bubbles in balance

(operations) and making sure the cash cycle is operating correctly, measuring profitability and resource (finance). If you're on a constant seesaw of *do* the work, *chase* the work, *do* the work, *chase* the work, with a small dose of cash flow crisis thrown in for good measure, chances are that your bubbles aren't in balance right now.

Let's think about this for a moment. When you get in your car, what's right in front of you? The dashboard, right? It gives you a visual indication of what's going on during your journey: are you going at the correct speed, do you have enough fuel, are there any warning lights? Sometimes you don't need to focus on *every* element of the dashboard. For example, if you've just filled up with petrol, you'll instinctively know how long you can drive for before you need to look at the fuel gauge again. You'll constantly need to be checking your speed, and be aware of any warning lights because that means something isn't working properly.

Why, then, wouldn't you have a dashboard for your business? The profit and loss account and the balance sheet provide great information, but they're *lagging* indicators. In other words, they're showing you a picture of what has *already* happened (like the rear-view mirror in your car). You can't do anything about that because it's in the past. Your dashboard, however, gives you an indication of what's *going* to happen: it provides *leading* indicators. What I mean is, if you come into a 30mph zone at 40mph and you check your dashboard as you see a speed camera approaching, you'll slow down. If you don't check your dashboard, the first sign you'll have of the speed camera's impact is in your rear-view mirror, after the fact.

What if we looked at it like this: the fuel gauge is your financial position. You've got to keep your cash flow tank topped up. The speedometer is your sales and marketing. It indicates how fast you're driving as a business. And the warning lights are operations. When something starts to go wrong in the engine or the mechanics of the vehicle, a light comes on to alert you.

Let's put these two ideas together: bubbles in balance and a business dashboard, and then roll forward to an image of you with "a commercial, profitable enterprise that works without you", sitting on a beach wondering how the business is performing. How many indicators would you need to see, and how regularly, to have enough confidence to sit back and order another pina colada because you knew that your business was performing as you'd expect?

You'd want a suite of maybe 12-15 measures representing the bubbles of sales and marketing, operations and finances, wouldn't you?

And, if you had someone reporting those key measures to you on a weekly basis, you could see the trends starting to emerge. In essence, wouldn't it be great to create a system in which you could catch any slippages early and do something about them?

One of the first things that I do with clients is implement a dashboard. While it takes a while to get right, any start is a good start. Measure the amount of leads and/or enquiries you receive on a weekly basis. If you're thinking right now that there's no point because you don't receive leads or enquiries on a weekly basis, then that is precisely the point of the dashboard. Your bubbles are out of balance!

Measure your conversion rate. Out of every 10 enquiries, how many do you win? Most people estimate this to be quite high… and then measure it to find something entirely different. What a fantastic opportunity! Many business owners will tell me the story that "my business is different", because quotes don't convert immediately and some even linger for a year or so. While that may be true, they're the exceptions (the 20%) and not the rule (the 80%). There is *always* a trend to be identified.

Operationally, your main performance indicators are about getting your product or service to your customer on time, on budget and to specification. How clear are you on your performance in that respect, right now? Depending on the complexity of your operations, there may only be a couple of operational indicators in your business.

Then measure your invoiced weekly sales, debtor balance (especially overdue debtors), and bank balance. Many people don't like looking at their bank balance. We'll call that denial! If it's on your dashboard, you've got to do something about it.

The big benefit of the dashboard is that it's an accountability mechanism. You see, if a number has to be reported on a weekly basis by someone in your business, they have to carry out the process to report it in the first place, so you now know that they are doing it.

When we place those numbers next to each other, on a weekly basis, over a period of time, it becomes very easy to not only see where the business is, but where it's going. On your dashboard, set a target for each of your performance indicators and measure yourself against it permanently. If you hit all of those indicators, what impact would that have on your business? How much more leverage would that give you with regards to time, team and money?

Get a dashboard now and become aware of those speed cameras.

Define at least three measures to reflect your:

- sales and marketing performance
- operational performance
- financial performance

Create a spreadsheet showing each of the categories you've defined. Allocate responsibility for each measure to a member of your team and collect that number each week. Also agree a target for each of the measures so that the team member has something clear to focus on. Record it on the dashboard to allow you to establish the trends emerging in your business.

Great. We're starting to get some transparency in relation to how your business runs. There's only one thing left to think about now, and that's how we start to create massive growth. That's the five ways, which we'll examine next and which ties neatly in with your dashboard.

The Five Ways – The Path to Profits and Freedom

I'd like to throw a final idea into the mix which draws all this together. While we are considering leverage, we should really discuss the most leveraged way to increase your profits, as presumably that's one of the main reasons you're in business: to make more money so you can have a better life and more freedom.

Now, I'm not going to discuss the 400 odd strategies out there to improve the profitability of your business. There are plenty of books out there to help you do that (*Instant Cashflow*[5], by Brad Sugars, teaches the strategies of how to leverage the five ways in detail, and I would recommend you buy it as a reference point).

Many of us would like more customers in our business. Most would like more turnover. Without exception, though, everyone wants more profit. Because, if you want more money, you need more profit.

But we can't get those things immediately: they're all results. Let me explain.

If we want to generate customers, we need to get leads (marketing effectiveness) and convert them (sales effectiveness).

Once we've got customers, we need to get them spending more (a higher average sales value), more often (increase the number of times each customer deals with us per year on average). This gives us our turnover.

Lastly, we need to make a margin to generate our profits.

When we consider building profit, we need to consider the five levers you can pull in your business to achieve that result.

---

[5] *Instant Cashflow*, Bradley J. Sugars, McGraw-Hill, 2005

Leads
X
Conversion rate %
=
Number of customers
X
Average sale value
X
Number of transactions
=
Turnover
X
Margin %
=
Profit

Figure 6.5: The 5 ways

The five ways are the elements in bold. They're the averages in your business right now. I understand that, for example, some customers will spend £10 each time they shop with you, and some will spend £1,000. I also get that some shop weekly and some once a year. We're looking for the averages, so that, eventually, we can drive them upwards by applying strategies and testing and measuring them.

Therefore, your five ways measures should absolutely appear on your dashboard.

Now, let's get clear: how many sets of five ways can you have in your business? As many as is useful.

To give you an example, I worked with an ecology business, who dealt with domestic clients and commercial clients. Of course, the spending patterns were completely different. For the domestic clients, leads were vital, as the average customer usually only needed one survey, and spent a relatively low amount. For commercial customers, the number of transactions and average sale was much higher. They generated five ways measures for each side of the business. It wouldn't have made sense for the business to have only one set of five ways numbers, as the average wouldn't have told them anything useful about their domestic or their commercial customers.

Also, different marketing strategies were required for each channel, as even though they were ostensibly buying the same service, we needed to talk to them about different things and in different ways.

Once we'd decided on the relevant five ways for the business, we started to measure them, regularly. The numbers went on a dashboard to identify the impact of the ideas we were trying in the business. When we found ideas that worked (and the dashboard told us so), we created a system for them, allocated responsibility and continued to measure to check for consistent performance and create accountability.

It's a very simple focus, but here's the thing: what if we were to focus on achieving a 10% increase in each of the five ways over the period of a year. Doesn't that sound achievable? Especially if your team are aligned, clear on the systems in place and making best use of their time.

If you were to achieve that 10%, what would the overall result be? By how much would your profit increase?

If you're thinking 10%, you couldn't be further from correct.

Remember, this is leverage: divide to multiply. More with less. Let's have a look at the numbers:

	Now	10% increase	Year 1	Year 5
Number of leads	4,000	400	4,400	6,442
x				
Conversion rate %	25.0%	2.5%	27.5%	40.3%
=				
Number of customers	1,000		1,210	2,594
x				
Average sale value	100	10	110	161
x				
Number of transactions	2	0.2	2.2	3.2
=				
Turnover	200,000		292,820	1,345,500
x				
Margin %	25.0%	2.5%	27.5%	40.3%
=				
Profit	50,000		80,525.50	541,735.30

Figure 6.6: The results of a 10% increase in the five ways

As you can see in figure 6.6 above, that's a 46% increase in turnover and a 61% increase in profit by the end of year one. And, if you continue to apply the same growth for five years, it's more than a 1,000% increase in profits.

The important thing here is not to get obsessed by the numbers, but by the concept. It's the idea of achieving small compounded gains which, when accumulated, create a much bigger gain. While you may not be able to take your margin from 25% to 40% over five years, you could probably increase your conversion rate by a far higher percentage and maybe take it from 25% to 60%, for example.

Now, of course, there is an order in which the five ways need to be applied. When I ask for input on this in seminars, the normal response is to drive number of leads first. In actual fact, that's normally the last thing we focus on.

First comes margins: we need to ensure that we know the margin on everything we sell. If we don't, we may be making losses we don't know about, or focusing on selling our least profitable items. Realistically, if we didn't know those numbers and started marketing unprofitable products, you could just market yourself out of business.

Next, we look at conversion rate because, in most businesses, they are getting more leads and enquiries than they are converting, which means they are leaving a lot of money on the table. If we focus on improving conversion rate, then the impact cascades down the other metrics in the business, so it's a huge win. If we double conversion, we double the business with no change in the number of leads.

Then we look at average sale. What's the easiest and quickest way to increase average sale value? Put your prices up. Normally, the idea of this strikes the fear of God into business owners, and a barrage of excuses come raining down as to all the reasons that they can't.

But, here's the thing: while there may be some products in your business which are highly price sensitive, I guarantee there are others which definitely are not. Consider when you go to the supermarket. You're probably reasonably aware how much a leg of lamb costs, for example, at Sainsbury's and Tesco. This is the key value item. But what about the mint sauce? I'm pretty sure you'll just buy that, whatever the price.

Where is the mint sauce in your business? There's the price increase opportunity if you can't do it across the board.

Fourth, we deal with number of transactions. How often are you talking with your customers right now? There's a well-researched statistic that states that the main reason customers leave you is "perceived indifference", meaning they don't feel cared about because they haven't been communicated with. How often are you *proactively* communicating with them at the moment?

The last place to focus is number of leads, in most cases. Why? For a number of reasons.

1. It's the part of the five ways which costs money to develop: marketing needs marketing spend, in most cases.
2. Every component other than the number of leads represents the internal mechanics of your business. You already own your sales process (conversion rate), and how much you charge, how often your customers come back and your margins. If you don't optimise these *before* you switch on your marketing, it could be like pouring sand through a sieve. Plug the holes in the areas of your business you already own before you start spending money to fuel an inefficient machine. The exception here would be if your business already spends a large amount on marketing and you're not clear which strategies are working and not working. In these cases, there are usually profit opportunities just by measuring this and turning off the marketing elements which are ineffective.

Now, I've mentioned that we have over 400 strategies across these five ways. But, think leverage again. Less is *always* more. Apply the 80:20 rule.

20% of the strategies will have 80% of the impact, and 20% of those will have 80% of *that* impact.

20% of 20% is 4%. And 4% of 400 is 16 strategies. That's about three strategies you have to find for each of the five ways, and you'll be home and dry!

What would be the impact on your business, 12 months from now, if you defined your five ways, measured them and then tested and measured strategies to improve them?, Imagine that, when you found the strategies that worked, you developed systems around them to create predictable consistency, hired someone and trained them in your system and then measured their performance to ensure you got the results you expected. How much more profit (and hence freedom) could you achieve in that time?

If you think I'm oversimplifying, then I'm going to propose that you may well be overcomplicating it. If you found the right three or four strategies and applied them consistently to the five ways, testing, measuring and then refining, does a 10% increase seem beyond the realms of possibility?

The answer is normally, "No". The reason we don't get the results is that we aren't consistent enough, or objective enough. And that inconsistency is created largely through the things we have discussed at length in this book. Lack of alignment, ownership and accountability, focus on the wrong tasks and unclear systems.

SUMMARY

We've seen, in this section, that the key to getting more from your business and your life lies in your systems and processes. The systems lay the foundation for the direction of the business and the accepted behaviour of team members, creating alignment – in other words, the "care" for your business. The systems provide the infrastructure and expected performance allowing you to manage (and your team to self-manage) to create true leverage in your business and to delegate with confidence.

Lay on top of that the principles of the five ways and you have a powerful vehicle to create the level of growth you want in your business. And there lies your path to true freedom and choice. It takes some work, but it's surely worth it, isn't it?

CONCLUSION

How much further are you on your journey towards life and business freedom?

Will you choose to address your own mindset, to be above the line most of the time, to put the fear aside and be open to new ideas?

Will you get really clear on your dreams and goals? Dreams and goals which give you the life that you really want.

Will you choose to really commit to those goals? So committed, in fact, that you can no longer do "stupid" in your business and choose to operate in your orange box most of the time.

Will you not only get your team above the line and focused on their most productive use of time, but also fully aligned with your goals and accountable for their own performance?

Will you choose to measure your activities so that your now high-performing team will innovate constantly to improve their own and, consequently, the overall performance of the business?

Because the smartest business owners take these learnings, apply them, and end up **getting MORE from their business, MORE freedom of choice in their lives, by thinking smarter and doing LESS.**

And you can too.

Wishing you all the best on your journey.

Enjoy!